I am so glad you are addressing Political Correctness. For a long time I have felt that it is having a detrimental effect on America's culture. You have explained *how*. Thank you so much. God bless you.

Dolores Self
Citizen and Homemaker

"America's Culture" captures not only the cultural beliefs on which our country was founded but offers a key to understanding their origin. Dr. McElroy's knowledge and experience in this subject provide a cogent explanation of what makes America an exceptional nation.

Charles Heller
Radio Host, "Liberty Watch"

John Harmon McElroy has written an admirable exposé of how Political Correctness is stifling free thought in our country, as it has in Marxist regimes. He exhibits a keen understanding of how America's unique culture promotes individual responsibility to achieve personal and societal success.

Paul Parisi
Director of Government Programs, 4Tucson

AMERICA'S CULTURE

Other books by
John Harmon McElroy

(editor) *The Life and Voyages of Christopher Columbus*
by Washington Irving

Finding Freedom: America's Distinctive Cultural Formation

*American Beliefs: What Keeps a Big Country
and a Diverse People United*

*The Sacrificial Years: A Chronicle of the Experiences
of Walt Whitman in the Civil War*

*Divided We Stand: The Rejection of American Culture
since the 1960s*

AMERICA'S CULTURE

Its Origins & Enemies

A Synopsis

John Harmon McElroy

50 States Press
2016

America's Culture Its Origins & Enemies, A Synopsis
is a publication of 50 States Press

First edition 2016

Copyright © 2015 by John Harmon McElroy

Manufactured in the United States of America by Arizona Lithographers, Tucson, AZ 85745. Designed and produced by Adam Colwell's WriteWorks LLC.

Information on purchasing may be obtained from 50 States Press, 2100 E. Speedway Blvd., #43661, Tucson, AZ 85733 and www.johnharmonmcelroy.com. Reduced prices are available for purchase in multiple quantities.

ISBN (print): 978-0-9892057-8-8
ISBN (eBook): 978-0-9969203-3-9
ISBN (eBook): 978-0-9969203-4-6

McElroy, John Harmon.
America's culture.
Includes index.
1. United States—Culture 2. National traits, American
3. Political Correctness.

ACKNOWLEDGMENTS

At the beginning, Lauren McElroy read the first chapter of this book, insightfully, when encouragement was most welcome. I also thank her for computer help and her careful checking of the book's quotations, citations, and accented words.

Al and Sally Litwak, as they have done before, favored me with a reading of the book's first complete draft and provided a perspicacious, detailed critique of its content and style at that stage of composition, for which I heartily thank them, as I do Clarence Stevens and Barney Brenner for meticulously proofing the final text.

Adam Colwell (Adam Colwell's WriteWorks, LLC) patiently guided me through the mysteries of electronic publishing which makes almost-instant publication possible—something much desired by an 81-year-old author. Mr. Colwell oversaw the entire process of the book's formatting, design, and production.

I thank Richard "Jake" Smart for his many stimulating conversations over the years and for telling me of *The American Patriot's Bible* which confirmed my assessment of the foundational importance of belief in God to America's culture.

As always, my accomplished wife provided me constant help of every kind. Ony's trustworthy, acute judgments have been the necessary supports of everything of worth I've ever done since that day, now long ago, when we married and became as the Book of Genesis says (2:24) "one flesh."

For
my beloved and loving Onyria

CONTENTS

Chapter One

INTRODUCTORY

The French Revolution in the eighteenth century and the communist revolutions of the twentieth century all intended the destruction of an existing culture and its replacement with a planned culture based on the philosophy of materialistic determinism. America's war with Britain in 1775-1783 was quite different. It was the defense of the God-centered culture that self-selected immigrants from many nations of Europe and their American-born descendants created, without plan or premeditation, on the Atlantic Coastal Plain of North America prior to the war to gain independence from Britain. This new culture, which had been formed during a period of eight generations under exceptional historical circumstances and geographic conditions, was "the American Revolution."

The culture's existence was announced to the world by the publication of the Declaration of Independence in 1776. Half a century later, the author of the Declaration's immortal phrase "all men are created equal" restated that belief of American culture in a letter explaining that illness would keep him from attending the celebrations of the Declaration's fiftieth anniversary. Thomas Jefferson said in this letter (the last of his life) that the Declaration meant that "the mass of mankind has not been born with saddles on their backs, nor a favored few booted and spurred, ready to ride them legitimately, by the grace of God."[1] That revolutionary cultural belief which Jefferson expressed for his fellow members of the Second Continental Congress and they signed at the risk of their lives represented a new way of life apart from the domination of kings and noblemen: a way of life in which all men by the grace of God have the same divine birthright to "Life, Liberty, and the Pursuit of Happiness" and government by "consent of the governed" and are equals in having those human rights in equal measure.

As the behaviors of generations of Americans were creating this revolutionarily new culture, the countries of Europe—including England—were obsessed by belief in social classes defined by birth. Men whose blood was "royal" and "noble" were born, Europeans culturally believed, to rule other men without such blood, who were to perform the manual labors their lowly birth mandated. Generations of wresting farms and towns from the North American wilderness for their own good and the improvement of their society, separated from the example of European cultural behavior by thousands of miles of ocean, led Americans to form such new cultural beliefs as *"Everyone must work and manual work is respectable;" "Society is a collection of persons* (not classes);" and *"Achievement rather than birth determines a person's social rank."*

One of the principal ways American culture diverged from Europe's culture regarded who was sovereign. As one historian of the American frontier has pointed out: "The first impulse of every new settlement, before land was cleared, cabins built, or stockade raised, was to hold a town meeting in which every man old enough to bear arms voted by majority rule for regulations

---

1 To Roger C. Weightman, June 24, 1826. *Thomas Jefferson Writings*, ed. Merrill D. Peterson (New York: Library of America, 1984), 1517.

governing social conduct, assignment of community tasks, and mutual defense" because "the new settlers were in most locations strangers to each other upon arrival, but ... were obliged to learn quickly to work together" to survive and prosper.[2] The compact the Pilgrims wrote and signed in 1620 for their "better Ordering and Preservation" while still on board their ship the Mayflower, before they went ashore to live in the wilderness of eastern Massachusetts, shows that this sort of initiative and self-reliance in government was part of American history from the beginning, which is why American independence was declared "in the Name, and by Authority of the good People of these Colonies" (the Declaration of Independence). The announcement to the world that the people of these former colonies of the king of England were sovereign and had a power from God to institute a government more suitable to them than their 169 years of subjection to British authority also announced that they were willing to sacrifice their lives and property in asserting that sovereignty.

The American belief in the sovereignty of the people of the States also manifested itself in writing, ratifying, and amending the Constitution of the United States. Delegations of representatives of the people of twelve of the thirteen States met in convention in Philadelphia and decided on provisions for a proposed written constitution for their general government. In making the many decisions on what should be in the proposed constitution, each State had one vote, regardless of its population, because the people of the States are equal in sovereignty. Virginia, then the most populous State, cast a single vote the same as the people of Delaware whose population was less than one-twelfth that of Virginia's. The ratification in 1787-1791 of

---

2 Dale Van Every, *Forth to the Wilderness: The First American Frontier* 1754-1774 (Arno Press, 1977), 305, and *A Company of Heroes: The American Frontier* 1775-1783 (Amo Press, 1977), 14-15.

the proposed Constitution of the United States and the adding of a Bill of Rights to it was accomplished by the same one-State-one-vote rule.

The sovereignty whereby the people of the States have made and altered their State constitutions and a general government for their Union exists only in the unity of the States with each other, as a nation, because only through that Union did any of them gain their independence from foreign rule. And that is why no State, or minority of States, can dissolve the Union by removing itself from it. For a state to rightfully secede would require an agreement of three-fourths of the States, the same majority that created and gave authority to the Union under the Constitution of the United States (Article VII).

George Washington summarized the American cultural belief in equal State sovereignty within the Union by saying: "The basis of our political systems is the right of the people to make and to alter their Constitutions of Government."[3] Washington's reference to "the people" is, we may be sure, to the people of the States rather than to the entire population of America, collectively considered, because otherwise his plural references to "political systems" and "constitutions" make no sense. In writing and approving constitutions for each State's government through their chosen representatives and doing the same for the general government of all the States, the people of the States of the United States have exercised their sovereignty. And just as the sovereignty of the people of Virginia and Delaware was equal when America's independence from British government was declared in 1776 and when the Constitution of the United States was written, ratified, and amended in 1787-1791, the sovereignty of the people of Wyoming, which is the smallest in population today, numbering a mere half a million, equals the sovereignty

---

3 "Farewell Address," September 19, 1796, *George Washington Writings*, ed. John Rhodehamel (Library of America, 1997), 968.

of the people of California, a State with more than 35 million inhabitants. For that same reason (equal State sovereignty) the Constitution of the United States is to this day amended by the one-State-one-vote rule and each State has the same number of representatives in the U. S. Senate. Equal State representation in the U. S. Senate is protected in the concluding clause of Article V in the Constitution, which indicates just how necessary equal State sovereignty is to the American form of government.

The book you have in hand is a synopsis, or profile, of America's exceptional culture and the exceptional conditions which produced it. The culture has three broad categories of beliefs regarding religion, government, and society, several of which are fundamental to America's free-market economy. The concluding chapter of the book discusses the hostile political forces which have been on the loose in the United States since the 1960s trying to replace America's historical culture with a planned culture based on the philosophy of materialistic determinism.

In making this synopsis of America's culture, the characteristics of the four major European areas of settlement in North and South America (Brazil, Canada, mainland Spanish America, and the United States of America) are compared to identify the exceptional features of America's culture. Since making comparisons is the best way to show the distinctiveness of a phenomenon, the relevant comparisons in this instance are to Brazil, Canada, and Spanish America because as former colonies of Europe on the mainland of North and South America, they have the most in common with the history and geography of the United States of America.

The overseas European imperialism which began with the fifteenth-century voyages of exploration sponsored by the Portuguese and Spanish crowns initiated the formation of the present-day cultures of Brazil, Canada, Spanish America, and the United States by bringing new populations to the American continents. Given the differences in the populations which began to develop after 1521 (the date of Spain's conquest of the Aztec civilization: the first permanent settlement of Europeans on the mainland of the Americas) and the differences in the geographies and colonial circumstances of these post-1521 societies in the Americas, a variety of new cultures began to develop on the North and South American mainland.

The enormous migration of free men and women from Europe to the mainland of the Americas during the past five centuries (the major portion of it to the United States), the much smaller forced migration of enslaved Africans to these continents in the first four of these centuries (the major portion of it to Brazil), and the free migrations from all over the world in the past two centuries constitute the largest movement of human beings in history. The kinds of migrations to Portuguese-ruled Brazil, French-ruled Canada, Spanish America, and the future United States during their colonial histories, the varied policies for governing these colonies, the diversely enculturated native populations the European colonizers encountered and interacted with in the New World, and the different geographies where the four colonizations occurred have been the principal factors in forming the four major post-1521 cultures in the Western Hemisphere.

But if we are to understand these distinctive cultural histories, we must of course first understand what culture is. A remark in a *New York Times* obituary on June 23, 2014 (page D14) that the deceased "loved American culture, particularly Hollywood movies, and especially Westerns" is useful to understanding this basic question because it epitomizes the common mistake nowadays of confusing popular culture with culture. The two are not the same. Popular culture is a society's tastes in entertainment, food, manners, and personal adornment which of course fluctuate from generation to generation and not uncommonly even within a generation. Popular culture is self-conscious and unstable. Culture, however, is stable; and its beliefs are normally acted on without the self-consciousness that characterizes popular culture.

Cultural beliefs are slow to form but once formed are long-lasting. They are the opposite of fashionable. Cultures have inertia. They resist change. Cultural beliefs unite all generations of a society. They even unite generations no longer alive with the living generations of a society. A culture serves the inherent human need for a common denominator of right behavior. Having such a denominator minimizes social conflict and makes it possible for human beings to live together in ongoing society.

Culture may be formally defined as a unique set of beliefs formed and transmitted through behavior from generation to generation. Cultures satisfy the deepest human need there is: to know moral right from moral wrong. That is an altogether different kind of concern from such ephemeral matters as whether to get a tattoo and what colors and design it should have and where to place it on the body, whether to get a tongue, lip, nostril, ear, or eyebrow piercing, or knowing the most up-to-date styles in music or what kind of clothing should be worn and manners adopted to be a member of the camp known as "cool"—the sorts of self-conscious concerns which typify popular culture.

The need to know moral right from moral wrong distinguishes human beings from other creatures. Our humanity requires us to live and act in society with other humans on the basis of some shared, stable set of belief-behaviors; and cultures serve that need by providing a right way to behave. A society's cultural beliefs and the behaviors which express them serve the natural interest every society has in maintaining itself as a society. In contrast to any other species, human beings have both a moral imagination and a propensity to *choose* to live in a wide range of geographies. These traits in conjunction with each other have produced an amazing variety of cultures.

Cultural beliefs are formed and transmitted by imitating the behaviors of the older generations of a society which embody them. As each successive generation comes of age and imitates their elders' conduct, this rising generation learns the cultural beliefs expressed in that behavior and thus participates in and perpetuates the culture. But only after a belief has been acted on for a minimum of four successive generations does it attain the historical validity that gives it cultural authenticity. To claim that a fondness for Western movies made in Hollywood is "American culture" is to confuse a taste for something trivial and transitory with something human beings must have to live together in society for many generations: namely a shared, internalized sense of right behavior.

Why are four generations needed for cultural beliefs to acquire their characteristic historical validity and compelling authority? The answer to that question requires us to examine how the sense of history arises among human beings. Let us suppose that a group of human beings has, for whatever reason, stayed together for four consecutive generations. It is the fourth generation of that incipient society which acquires the sense of history that is essential to a culture's validity and authority, because the fourth generation comes of age without personal knowledge of their great-grandparents: the initial generation of the group which has died off leaving behind their children (the grandparents of the fourth generation) and that generation's children (the parents of the fourth generation). The fourth generation acquires a sense of history—that is to say, the sense of a way of life before they were born—through hearing stories told by their parents and grandparents about the first generation, which those generations (the second and third) knew but the fourth generation did not. The reverence manifested in these stories for the no-longer-present generation, plus other signs of respect for the dead, convey to the fourth generation the sense that the conduct of their parents and grandparents (which they are beginning to emulate) belongs to a historical way of life. As more generations come of age, act, grow old, and die, leaving behind further generations of descendants, the historical sense in that society grows stronger.

Once a society has formed a set of historical beliefs through this process, a culture exists, and its authority can supersede the blood kinship which may be assumed to constitute the basis for all primitive human groups. A set of historical belief-behaviors is as effective in attaining social unity for a group of human beings as the blood ties of clan membership. Eight generations— another complete repetition of the four-generation behavioral cycle—may be required to form a fully compelling set of cultural beliefs.

Culture, then, is essentially a set of right beliefs which are right because they are historical. The shortest definition of culture is this: Historically Validated Right Behavior.

The formation of a culture resembles the formation of a path. The first person to traverse a landscape decides how to go through it by making choices among plausible alternative routes. Travelers who come along after the pathfinder tend to follow in the track of his decisions for two reasons: one, it's easier to follow a discernible track than to make an entirely new path; second, the pathfinder's choices will have practical value. As time passes and more and more travelers use the path, it becomes so plain and smooth that it acquires a compelling authority as the way to go through that landscape. A path is a way to go that has physical utility; a culture is a way to live that has social utility. A culture is the way of life which the behavior of many generations of a society has endowed with moral authority.

Over time, of course, the conditions in which a culture has

formed may change, and over long stretches of time they surely will. But this does not mean the beliefs of a culture must all be changed as the conditions in which the culture exists change. Constant change would defeat the purpose cultures serve, which is to satisfy the human yearnings for social unity and moral stability. The natural response to changing conditions is to find some new behavior or to modify some existing behavior which can continue to express the historically validated beliefs of a culture. For instance, the advent in the United States in the nineteenth century of industrialization and urbanization represented fundamental changes for a society whose circumstances during its formation had been overwhelmingly rural and agrarian. Urbanization and industrialization did not, however, change America's set of cultural beliefs, because work in factories and offices expressed as satisfactorily as farm and shop work the cultural belief that everyone must work. A culture changes by slowly discontinuing an existing belief or adding a new one.

Before proceeding to the descriptions and discussions that will profile the beliefs of American culture, a few more comments on the nature of culture are necessary. The first of these in importance is the observation that cultural beliefs have to be simple: *The people of the States have equal sovereignty; Organization is essential to improving society;* etc. If cultural beliefs were complicated, they would not be clear to even the dullest members of a society. Without the kind of simplicity that distinguishes them, cultural beliefs could not be transmitted intact from generation to generation through the behaviors which express them and so would lose their coherence. Only simple beliefs can be acted on by enough people for enough successive generations (the minimum number, remember, is four) to acquire the historical validity and compelling authority that make them cultural beliefs.

But if cultural beliefs have to be simple, why then do we so often say a culture is complex? The answer to this is that a culture's complexity lies in the *set* of its beliefs, not in the beliefs that comprise the set. Such complexity applies even to cultures classified as primitive. (When it comes to culture, the set of beliefs of a primitive culture is as complex as more recent cultures.) The same is true of a culture's uniqueness: it is the *set* of a culture's beliefs that is unique, not every belief in the set. Though some beliefs of a culture will in all likelihood occur in that culture only and no other, it would probably be safe to say that for every belief in a culture to be unique, it would have to have been formed on some other planet. In saying a culture is complex or unique, one is saying that the set of its beliefs is complex or unique.

Here is an example of a historical behavior that expresses a cultural belief.

The amount of time required for the four major areas of European settlement on the mainland of North and South America—Brazil, Canada, the mainland nations of Spanish America, and the United States—to become independent of European rule is an index of the cultural value that self-governing behavior has in these societies. A comparison of how quickly each major area of European colonization in the Western Hemisphere became independent of European rule and self-governing reveals that the United States took just *eight* generations (1607-1776: 169 years). Canada required *nineteen* generations (1608-1982: 374 years). Spain ruled the mainland nations of Spanish America for *fifteen* generations (1521-1824: 303 years, and the three island nations of Spanish America for another seventy-five years). Brazil was under Portuguese rule for *fourteen* generations (1532-1822: 290 years).

Canada did not become fully independent of Europe until control over the Canadian constitution was transferred from London to Ottawa by an act of the British Parliament and signed into law by the British monarch in 1982. This act giving Canadians ultimate and complete say in their governance is known in Canadian history as the "Repatriation of the Constitution." Nonetheless, under Canada's repatriated constitution the British monarch remains the Head of State of Canada's government and her image continues to appear on Canadian money.

An even more pronounced European cultural presence persisted in Brazil for three generations after its independence from Portugal was proclaimed in 1822. The crown prince of Portugal made that proclamation because his father, the king, in returning to Lisbon from the royal family's temporary asylum in their principal colony, left him in charge of Brazil with the advice that should a Brazilian declaration of independence appear imminent to make a preemptive announcement of separation and create a monarchy of Portuguese royal blood. Under a constitution which this European scion of royal blood had to approve as "Emperor of Brazil," the title he chose for himself, monarchical government lasted in Brazil until 1889, when it was finally rejected and a republic was established.

The precocious independence the United States manifested—two centuries sooner than Canada and a century and a quarter sooner than Brazil and Spanish America—was therefore exceptional cultural behavior, which is why the United States is the only nation in the Western Hemisphere to have been independent of European rule longer than it was a colonial dependency. Brazil and Spanish America will not reach that point in their histories for another century; Canada will not reach it until the middle of the twenty-fourth century.

One further observation. The beliefs of our own culture are so engrained in the way we think and act that we are normally unaware of them. Only persons who reside for a time in another culture become conscious of their own culture. Thus, Thomas Jefferson, after having traveled in Europe before settling down to his duties in France as U. S. ambassador, wrote from Paris to his friend James Monroe in America:

I sincerely wish you may find it convenient to come here. The pleasure of the trip will be less than you expect but the utility greater ... My God! How little do my country men know what precious blessings they are in possession of, and which no other people on earth enjoy. I confess I had no idea of it myself.[4]

In the following century, Ralph Waldo Emerson similarly remarked of Americans who sojourned in Europe as he had that they are "Americanized" (his word). In the twentieth century, the American writer James Baldwin was acknowledging the same thing in saying of an American expatriate like himself: "From the vantage point of Europe, he discovers his own country."[5] This was likewise my experience in Europe in 1968-1969 as a Fulbright Professor of American Studies at the University of Salamanca in Spain. Only then did I become conscious of the distinctiveness of my cultural beliefs and begin to take a serious (and as it turns out an abiding) interest in the question of cultural differences and their origins.

---

4 Jefferson to Monroe, June 17, 1785, *Thomas Jefferson Writings*, 808.
5 James Baldwin, "A Question of Identity," an essay in *Notes of a Native Son, with a New Introduction by the Author* (Beacon Press, 1984), 137.

Chapter Two

AMERICA IS A
CHOSEN COUNTRY

Only the presidents of the United States and their standbys, the vice-presidents, are elected by the people of all the States. Because of the singular way the president attains his office, he is the only legitimate individual spokesman for the people of the entire country, and the most solemn occasion on which he speaks in that capacity is the address he makes immediately after being publicly sworn into office. In these public addresses, the chief magistrate of the United States invariably makes some sort of reference to God and often speaks of God's providential involvement with America's history. These professions of faith in a higher power than man began with the first president elected under the Constitution of the United States.

George Washington's First Inaugural Address invoked God as "the Almighty Being who rules over the Universe," "the Great Author of every public and private good," "the benign Parent of the human race," and "the invisible hand, which conducts the Affairs of men." Washington also told his fellow Americans attending his inauguration that "every step, by which they [the United States] have advanced to the character of an independent nation, seems to have been distinguished by some token of providential agency." In his first public act as president, Washington also made reference to the Ten Commandments when he said, regarding the Creator, that "the propitious smiles of Heaven can never be expected on a nation that disregards the eternal rules of order and right, which Heaven itself has ordained." He concluded the Address by beseeching God to bless him and his fellow officers in the general government with wisdom, temperance, and "enlarged views."[1]

Washington—who had also been elected to command the American army in the War for Independence and to preside over the Convention that wrote the Constitution of the United States—often expressed in private letters his judgment that in drafting the new constitution, "It was indeed next to a Miracle that there should have been so much unanimity...."[2] Washington likewise characterized America's victory in its War for Independence as miraculous. Regarding the war and the writing of the Constitution of the United States, he knew better than any other American the odds against success, and in his opinion only divine intervention could account for the outcome of these events. Rod Gragg's book *By the Hand of Providence: How Faith Shaped the American Revolution*, a comprehensive account of the American belief in providence in reference to winning the war with Britain, vividly summarizes the odds against an American victory.[3] The book also analyzes Washington's assessment of the essential role God had in determining the war's outcome.

It was not just in his First Inaugural Address or in his personal correspondence, however, that we find the first president of the United States expressing a belief in divine intervention. Seven of his eight constitutionally-required annual messages to Congress mention God's providence and attribute America's

---

1 *George Washington Writings*, 730-34.
2 To Catharine Macaulay Graham, Ibid., 752.
3 (Howard Books, 2011), 5-8.

"prosperity"—an eighteenth-century synonym for success—to "the Ruler of the Universe." Given Washington's belief that God had a hand in American history, he frequently expressed, as Americans often have, "profound gratitude to the Author of all good, for the numerous, and extraordinary blessings we [Americans] enjoy."[4]

Atheists may scoff at the idea that America is under God's special care as mere pandering for the religious vote, but such cynicism is misplaced. The point is that Americans generally and American presidents in particular, in Washington's day and since, have believed that God has exerted his almighty power in American history. If cynics were correct and the frequent assertions by American presidents of God's providential concern for America were nothing but politicking for votes, why did Washington assert the belief so often in private letters to friends and in his annual messages to Congress? Even more significantly, why are some of the most moving personal affirmations of belief in God and his providential relationship to America by American presidents found in their *second* inaugural addresses, when there was no prospect of further election to the highest office of government in the United States?

Without a doubt, the most moving inaugural address ever delivered by an American president is Lincoln's Second Inaugural Address which is replete with allusions to God's providence. It articulates with utmost conviction and biblical eloquence Lincoln's belief that God was permitting the American Civil War to continue, year after blood-smeared year, to chastise Americans with an iron rod for having allowed two centuries of chattel slavery in the United States in transgression of America's cultural belief that God has endowed all human beings with the

---

4 *George Washington Writings*, 978, 919, 887, 832, 846, 786-87, 749. Gragg's *By the Hand of Providence* is a comprehensive account of the American belief in Providence in regard to winning the War for Independence.

same birthright of freedom. In his Second Inaugural Address, Abraham Lincoln quoted or paraphrased five passages from the Bible.[5]

In his Second Inaugural Address, President Jefferson held forth on the subject of God's involvement in American history in a language reminiscent of many a sermon on God's providence from seventeenth-century New England pulpits. In this 1805 Inaugural Address, Thomas Jefferson expressed his hope of success as president in these terms:

> I shall need ... the favor of that Being in whose hands we are, who led our forefathers, as Israel of old, from their native land, and planted them in a country flowing with all the necessaries and comforts of life; who has covered our infancy with his providence and our riper years with his wisdom and power; and to whose goodness I ask you to join with me in supplication that he will so enlighten the minds of your servants, guide their councils, and prosper their measures, that whatsoever they do, shall result in your good, and shall secure to you the peace, friendship, and approbation of all nations.[6]

In publicly proclaiming these religiously-wrought sentiments at his second inauguration, Jefferson had no need to garner votes.

When Franklin Delano Roosevelt took office as president in 1933 and delivered his First Inaugural Address, he rather perfunctorily remarked at the end of it: "...we humbly ask the blessing of God. May he protect each and every one of us. May He guide me in the days to come."[7] But at his fourth inaugural, after having confronted for twelve years not only the challenges

---

5   *Lincoln: Selected Speeches and Writings*, ed. Don E. Fehrenbacher (Library of America, 1989), 449-50.

6   *Thomas Jefferson Writings*, 523.

7   *Inaugural Addresses of the Presidents of the United States From George Washington to Richard Milhous Nixon 1973*, 93rd Congress, 1st Session, House Document 93-208 (United States Government Printing Office, 1974), 239.

of the Great Depression but the far greater tribulations of simul-taneously fighting two major wars—one in the far reaches of the seas and islands of the Pacific and the other on the opposite side of the globe in the Atlantic, North Africa, and Europe—Roosevelt expressed a reverence for God's providence which was anything but perfunctory. Near the beginning of that final inau-gural address of his twelve-year presidency, he remarked that he and the audience he was addressing were "in the presence of our God" and that he was conscious of having just taken the oath of his office in God's presence. He concluded his brief remarks by saying:

> The Almighty God has blessed our land in many ways. He has given our people stout hearts and strong arms with which to strike mighty blows for freedom and truth. He has given to our country a faith which has become the hope of all peoples in an anguished world. So we pray to Him now for the vision to see our way clearly—to see the way that leads to a better life for ourselves and for all our fellow men—to the achievement of His will, to peace on earth.[8]

The fifty-five presidential inaugural addresses contain over two hundred expressions of belief in God and allusions to his providence. Some of these expressions have been surprisingly personal. Presidents Dwight D. Eisenhower and George H. W. Bush, both veterans of World War II—the former as Supreme Allied Commander in Europe and the latter as a young Navy pilot in the Pacific—made personal prayers.

Eisenhower opened his First Inaugural Address: "My friends, before I begin the expression of those thoughts that I deem appropriate to this moment, would you permit me the privilege of uttering a little private prayer of my own. And I ask that you

---

8 Ibid., 248-49.

bow your heads." In the prayer he then made, he asked God to bless him and those appointed to advise him in the executive branch of the government to "the service of the people in this throng, and their fellow citizens everywhere" and to give him and those who were going to serve with him "the power to discern clearly right from wrong, and allow all our words and actions to be governed" by that perception so "all may work for the good of our beloved country and Thy glory. Amen."[9]

Thirty-six years later, in 1989, after being sworn into office, George H. W. Bush said: "My first act as President is a prayer—I ask you to bow your heads. Heavenly Father, we bow our heads and thank You for Your love. Accept our thanks for the peace that yields this day and the shared faith that makes its continuance likely. Make us strong to do Your work, willing to heed and hear Your will, and write in our hearts these words: 'Use power to help people.' For we are given power not to advance our own purposes nor to make a great show in the world, nor a name. There is but one just use of power and it is to serve people. Help us remember, Lord. Amen."[10]

In January of 1961, President Eisenhower at the end of his two-term presidency made a nationally televised farewell address to the nation in which he said:

> ...America is today the strongest, the most influential and most productive nation in the world. Understandably proud of this pre-eminence, we yet realize that America's leadership and prestige depend, not merely upon our unmatched material progress, riches and military strength, but on how we use our power in the interests of world peace and human betterment. Throughout America's adventure in free government, our basic purposes have been to keep the peace; to foster progress

---

9 Ibid., 257.
10 *New York Times*, January 21, 1989, A10.

in human achievement, and to enhance liberty, dignity and integrity among peoples and among nations. To strive for less would be unworthy of a free and religious people.[11]

We Americans have been, as Eisenhower said, a "religious people," not in the sense of being extraordinarily pious or having a one-hundred-percent church attendance on Sundays, but as a people who are firm in the belief generation after generation that God Almighty, the Creator, exists and has blessed us with a great country divinely destined for a great and benevolent mission in his Creation.

We have believed, as that quintessential American Benjamin Franklin did, in "one God, Creator of the Universe. That he governs it by his Providence. That he ought to be worshipped. That the most acceptable Service we render to him is doing good to his other Children. That the soul of Man is immortal, and will be treated with Justice in another life respecting its Conduct in this."[12] Franklin's "Creed," as he called it, is probably as good a summary as any of our faith as a nation of believers, with more religious denominations and more tolerance for them than any nation in the world. He was eighty-four when he articulated it. His earliest views on God's government of the universe are contained in his essay "On the Providence of God in the Government of the World." Franklin was twenty-four when he wrote that essay.[13]

Another veteran of World War II who became president, John Fitzgerald Kennedy, stated in his inaugural address his firm belief in God's existence and providence by emphatically

---

11 *A Documentary History of the United States: An Expanded Edition*, ed. Richard D. Heffner (New American Library, 1965), 313.

12 To Ezra Stiles, March 9, 1790. *Benjamin Franklin Writings*, ed. J.A. Leo Lemay (Library of America, 1987), 1179.

13 Ibid., 163-168.

declaring "The rights of man come not from the generosity of the state, but from the hand of God."[14]

These convictions by Eisenhower, George H. W. Bush, and Kennedy echo the general conviction among American combat veterans of World War II who like my father, Major John H. McElroy, the executive officer of the 341st Field Artillery Battalion of the 89th Infantry Division in Patton's Third Army, referred to America as "God's Country." Denis Brogan, a twentieth-century British academic who specialized in U.S. history and made frequent visits to America, remarked on this American belief: "Deep in the American mind [is] a belief that his is God's Country" and that belief, he said, is "a sacred truth."[15]

Americans have long believed that God has intended America to be a self-governing and prosperous republic, an example to the world of a more abundant, freer way of life. As many American patriots have said, God has blessed America and made it the greatest example of freedom and prosperity in human history. President Ronald Reagan especially was fond of speaking of America as "a shining city upon a hill" beaming the light of liberty on the world. "Freedom is the very essence of our nation," he said. "To be sure, ours is not a perfect nation, but even with our troubles, we remain the lesson of hope for oppressed people everywhere.... God intended America to be free, to be the golden hope of mankind."[16]

The fact that more immigrants have chosen America as their destination than any other place in the world is the most important single fact of American history and the surest proof that America is indeed a chosen country. To its inhabitants, who believe God has chosen America to exemplify a new way of life for

---

14 *Inaugural Addresses*, 267.

15 *U.S.A.: An Outline of the Country, Its People and Institutions* (Oxford University Press, 1941), 70.

16 *The Wit and Wisdom of Ronald Reagan*, ed. James C. Humes (Regnery Publishing, 2007) 205, 5, 6.

mankind and has endowed their country with extraordinary blessings to make it attractive to persons seeking a better way of life, America has been throughout its history and continues to be a chosen country. The many tens of millions of immigrants who have come to America in pursuit of happiness were choosing not just a new homeland for themselves and their offspring but affirming their God-given right to be free. America has been, in other words, a gathering place for believers in God's freedom. Being an American is not a matter of birthplace or color. It is a matter of believing in rights that come from God and respecting other persons because they have those same rights in equal measure.

President Lincoln identified God's mission for America in the address he made at Gettysburg in 1863 honoring the deaths of those Americans who, in the great battle there, gave "the last full measure of devotion" to preserve the Union of States. Lincoln told his listeners the United States was "conceived in liberty and dedicated to the proposition that all men are created equal." He also said that the war then engulfing the country would decide whether "any nation so conceived and so dedicated" could long endure and whether the sacrifices of life and limb in the war to preserve the Union were being made in vain or would lead to "this nation, under God, [having] a new birth of freedom," so that "government of the people, by the people, for the people, shall not perish from the earth."[17]

Equal freedom under God's law (Washington's "eternal rules of order and right") and the blessing of a republican form of government constituted by the people of the States who have agreed to live under it is God's will for America and through the example of America God's will for all mankind. World War II magnified the renown of that example. Through America's unifying leadership and its role as "the arsenal of democracy" in World War II, which

---

17 *Lincoln: Selected Speeches and Writings*, 405.

may be viewed as a struggle between the good that God wills for the world and the evil that man creates by using his God-given freedom to defy God's will, America became known throughout the world in 1942-1945 as a great and powerful leader of the free nations of the world. Before World War II, only half a dozen countries had a government like America's, which was the first nation to write and approve a constitution for government through representatives of the people who would live under it. After the war, many countries imitated America's government.

Americans are proud of the fact that more persons have chosen to immigrate to their country than have ever gone anywhere else in human history. But the evil of the slavery that existed in America from the 1660s to the 1860s proves that some persons in America were being denied their God-given equal birthright of freedom and the pursuit of the opportunities it offers and were being forced to labor for the betterment of their masters rather than their own. The three Civil War amendments to the Constitution (the Thirteenth, Fourteenth, and Fifteenth ratified in 1865-1870) were intended to be the "new birth of freedom" Lincoln envisioned by acknowledging the right of black Americans to participate in the better way of life God has willed for human beings.

In 1963, one hundred years after Lincoln's speech at Gettysburg, Martin Luther King Jr., a Baptist pastor, spoke to an immense crowd of people in front of the Lincoln Memorial in Washington, and via radio and television to Americans everywhere. He reminded America that though black Americans had been freed from the condition of being property (an inhuman status that once justified for some Americans taking away their God-given birthrights), black Americans did not yet actually enjoy the full and equal rights those three constitutional amendments were meant to confer on them.[18] The next year,

---

18 "I Have A Dream," *A Testament of Hope: The Essential Writings of Martin Luther King, Jr.* ed. James Melvin Washington (Harper & Row, 1986), 217-20.

in furtherance of the equality spoken of in the Declaration of Independence and the color-blind society Martin Luther King envisioned, Congress passed and President Lyndon Johnson signed the Civil Rights Act of 1964 banning racial inequities in public accommodations and employment.

What kind of place was America when Jamestown was settled, 115 years after Columbus's first voyage to the Americas, that caused so many persons from around the world to want to come to it in the next four centuries?

Geographically, America at the time of its beginnings as a place of European colonization was a 1,200-mile-long coastal plain defined by the Atlantic Ocean and the foothills of the Appalachian Mountains. When the first Europeans colonized this coastal plain, it was a Stone Age wilderness covered mostly by the forest that started growing there after the passing of the last Ice Age in North America 10,000 years ago. To persons crossing the Atlantic to America, the plain first appears as an almost invisible, thin line on the horizon, barely distinguishable from the distant waves. In the 1600s, the springtime fragrance of the forest's myriad aromatic and flowering trees, mixed with the pungent smell of the sun-warmed resins and needles of its innumerable pine trees, could be detected half a day's sail out to sea, long before the land itself came into view. The spaciousness of this cradle of American culture is perhaps best measured by the fact that three of the present-day States of the United States formed from the Atlantic Coastal Plain of North America and its adjacent foothills and mountains exceed in area England's 50,352 square miles of territory: Georgia with 59,441 square miles, New York with 54,475, and North Carolina with 53,821.[19]

European settlers in this wilderness found an abundance of chestnuts and other wild foods and a super-abundance of fine

---

19 *Cosmopolitan World Atlas, Revised Edition* (Rand McNally, 1996), 257-59.

woods for building, fabrication, and heating. Wild grapevines as thick as a man's thigh entwined some of the ancient trees, and along the coast were thick-stemmed seaside grasses taller than a man. There were innumerable creeks, many rivers bigger than the biggest river of England, lots of springs of pure water, and a good many marshes, swamps, ponds, and meadows. Big wild animals (bear, moose, deer, elk, woodland bison) and their predators (wolves and cougars) inhabited this primeval landscape along with plenty of smaller game, and there were no manorial lords to prohibit a man from partaking of this plenteous natural bounty.

In the middle of the coastal plain was a 200-mile-long bay (the Chesapeake) encompassing 3,000 square miles of sheltered salt water into which the Susquehanna, the Potomac, the Rappahannock, and many lesser rivers copiously poured fresh water. Numerous tidal estuaries and broad sounds protected from the ocean by elongated barrier islands provided the sailing ships of that era good anchorages. Along the shores of this coast were numerous beds of giant oysters and beaches where fat clams abounded. In the colder northern waters of the coast were abundant lobsters and immense fisheries of succulent codfish. During the spring and autumn waterfowl migrations, the concentrations of ducks, geese, and swans were so immense it could take an hour for the last bird in a flock rising from the water to become airborne. The springtime spawning runs of fish could fill creeks bank-to-bank.

My grandfather Edward Wagner—the oldest son of a German immigrant who had been brought as a child to America—who was born and raised in the late 1800s in the same rural town in western Pennsylvania where I was born and raised, told me that he had seen in his youth farmers back wagons into a stream and using pitchforks fill them with fish to spread on their fields to plow under for fertilizer. He also told me of having seen flights of passenger pigeons so immense they blocked the light of the sun and heavy-bodied sturgeon as long as a man is tall taken from the Allegheny River. Such recollections suggest the tremendous abundance of natural resources on the Atlantic Coastal Plain of North America that had attracted European settlers.

Earlier, more telling inventories of those natural resources can be found in chapters XLIII and XLVII of Richard Hakluyt, *Voyages and Discoveries: The Principal Navigations, Voyages, Traffiques and Discoveries of the English Nation* (Penguin Books, 1985); Capt. John Smith, Vol. I, *Travels and Works* (Burt Franklin, 1967); John Bakeless, *The Eyes of Discovery. North America as Seen by the First Explorers* (J. B. Lippincott, 1961); and William Bartram, *Travels Through North & South Carolina, Georgia, East & West Florida, the Cherokee Country, the Extensive Territories of the Muscogulges or Creek Confederacy, and the Country of the Chactaws*, ed. Thomas P. Slaughter (Library of America, 1996), first published in Philadelphia in 1791.

America's most attractive natural resource for Europeans was its abundance of plow land (arable land). After the forest was cleared, large parts of the coastal plain could be converted to farms. West of the Appalachians lay still more arable land, both forested and treeless, all the way to the far-off Mississippi River: the immense territory which American negotiators at the Paris peace conference ending the War for Independence acquired for the United States, a territory larger than any country of Europe but Russia. Beyond the Mississippi lay the seemingly endless continental expanse of untilled prairies called the Great Plains, which the United States acquired title to from France through purchase in 1803, twenty years after the War for Independence.

Free persons from Europe immigrating to this part of North America were coming to the only temperate space of continental dimensions in the Americas which had a potential for human habitation and utilization from ocean to ocean. Nowhere else in the Western Hemisphere was there such an abundance of arable land and a temperate climate. And while geography certainly does not in itself provide a sufficient explanation for why particular cultures develop, geography does affect what human beings can do in a particular place over time, and therefore what sort of culture they can develop through their behavior generation by generation in that place. History shows man shaping his environment, whatever it may be. But particular climates, terrains, and resources constitute the physical framework within which man's creative energies and moral imagination must operate and develop.

To be sure, Canada and Brazil at the beginning of their European settlement were also Stone Age wildernesses of continental dimensions. But Canada and Brazil were arctic and equatorial wildernesses hostile to thorough, large-scale development by human beings. Moreover, these areas of European colonization and Spanish America were governed by colonial policies which had a large influence on the kind of post-1521 cultures that developed in them in comparison to the future United States of America.

Canada is the largest country of the Western Hemisphere, with 3.85 million square miles compared to 3.79 million square miles for the United States, which has the largest population of any of the Hemisphere's nations. Canada's geography, however, has prevented it from acquiring the population its great size would suggest it should have. (The continents of Europe, with 3.8 million square miles, and Australia, with 3.0 million square miles, are both smaller than Canada, the world's second-largest nation after the Russian Federation with 6.6 million square miles.[20]) Canada's extraordinary profusion of lakes, rivers, steams, ponds, and bogs (the watery terrain left by the melting of the mile-thick Ice Cap that once covered northern North

---

20 *The World Almanac and Book of Facts 2015,* 760, 848.

America) plus its boreal latitudes dictate that most of Canada is locked in the solid grip of ice most of the year. Because so much of this vast nation is inimical to human settlement on a large scale, much of it remains to this day in the same condition it was in at the time of Columbus's first voyage to the Western Hemisphere. Less than 5 percent of Canada has been developed into farmland; its density of population is a mere 9.9 persons per square mile, and its total number of inhabitants remains below 35 million. On the other hand, the United States, with its temperate climate and larger portion of arable land (17 percent), has a population density of 90.3 persons per square mile and over 310 million inhabitants.[21]

Brazil's heartland is the Amazon Basin, a colossal network of equatorial and tropical rivers, parts of which receive twelve feet of rain a year, which contains an estimated two-thirds of all the planet's river waters. The first European to discover the Amazon River did so while attempting to find the source of the current of fresh water he encountered on the open ocean (the Amazon's stupendous discharge of water into the Atlantic). While thus engaged, he left the ocean without knowing it because the Amazon at its mouth is so wide that from the deck of a small ship in midstream both banks of the river *disappear below the curvature of the earth.* The volume of water in this river and its tributaries is like no other river basin on earth, which is why Brazilians call the Amazon "O Rio Mar" (the river-sea) to convey some sense of its unique immensity. (The Amazon's undredged main channel is so deep ocean freighters can go all the way across northern Brazil to the river port of Iquitos in Peru.) The annual floods of this river-system inundate an area comparable to the Mediterranean, the planet's largest inland sea.

Because of the Amazon Basin's implacable watery reality

---

21 *Cosmopolitan World Atlas,* 257, 259.

and other forbidding features (such as its considerable number of insect species having bites harmful to humans), only a small fraction of Brazil's population of over 200 million inhabits this heartland of South America's largest nation. Most Brazilians still reside within 300 miles of the Atlantic, south of the coastal city of Salvador in the direction of the country's more inviting subtropical and temperate states of Guanabara, Sao Paulo, Minas Gerais, Parana, Santa Catarina, and Rio Grande do Sul. Brazil's 3.3 million square miles is somewhat larger than the forty-eight contiguous States of the United States. But its percentage of arable land (8.5 percent) is only half that of the U. S. Its density of population is 61.5 persons per square mile.[22]

Because of the forbidding topography of much of Brazil's interior, it took Brazilians more than four centuries from the time of its first European coastal settlement to build the inland capital city they had long wanted to build to attract settlers inland. Begun in the 1950s and dedicated in 1960, the new capital (Brasilia) is on a grassy upland well south of the Amazon Basin and 600 miles in from the Atlantic, a site which was largely uninhabited ranchland in 1950. (Six hundred miles is the distance from New York City to Cincinnati, Ohio.)

As for mainland Spanish America, its sixteen nations— Mexico, Guatemala, Honduras, El Salvador, Nicaragua, Costa Rica, and Panama in North and Central America and Colombia, Venezuela, Ecuador, Peru, Bolivia, Chile, Argentina, Uruguay, and Paraguay in South America—comprise the Western Hemisphere's largest and most populous cultural area (4.3 million square miles; 359 million inhabitants).[23] Spanish America is also uniquely mountainous. All but two of the Spanish-speaking nations of South America straddle the 5,000-mile-long cordillera

---

22 *The World Almanac and Book of Facts 2015*, 757.
23 These figures on the area and population of mainland Spanish America are the totals for these sixteen nations in *The World Almanac and Book of Facts 2015*.

of immense mountains in the western part of that continent, which has a great many peaks over 20,000 feet and is the earth's longest chain of high mountains, second only to the Himalayas in elevation. Following an abrupt lowering at Panama, the lands of Spanish America begin to rise again and gradually ascend to high mountains across the center of Mexico. Thus, most of the 8,000-mile, north-south distance of Spanish America is mountainous. Five important cities in Spanish America: La Paz (Bolivia), Cuzco (Peru), Quito (Ecuador), Bogota (Colombia), and Mexico City have elevations respectively of 12,000, 11,300, 9,300, 8,600, and 7,800 feet, the latter being the fourth-largest city in the world after Tokyo, Delhi, and Shanghai.

Unlike Brazil, Canada, and the United States, mainland Spanish America has an elongated shape. Its 8,000-mile, north-south distance attains a 1,000-mile width at only two places: side-by-side Colombia and Venezuela and side-by-side Chile, Argentina, and Uruguay. Because of its mountainous terrain and extremely elongated shape, mainland Spanish America was liberated from European rule in segments: Mexico and Central America, northern and west-central South America, and southern South America. Simon Bolivar, the liberator of the largest portion ("some three million square miles") of this far-flung territory rode "at least twenty thousand miles on horseback" in the early nineteenth century during his decade of campaigning against the military forces of imperial Spain.[24] (Francisco de Miranda, Jose de San Martin, Bernardo O'Higgins, and Antonio Jose de Sucre were other prominent Creole military leaders who liberated large areas of South America from Spanish rule.) It was never likely (geographically speaking) that one political entity could have been made from this elongated region of the Americas, though that was the fondest hope of Bolivar's most

---

24 Robert Harvey, *Liberators: Latin America's Struggle for Independence* (Overlook Press, 2000), 227.

heroic efforts for at least northern South America (Colombia, Ecuador, and Venezuela), the region of his birth.

A unique historical fact also distinguishes mainland Spanish America. At the time of its European colonization, it had the only civilizations in the Americas, defining civilization as permanently occupied large cities surrounded by ample agricultural production. In the early 1500s, tens of millions of human beings lived along the coasts of this part of the Americas and in the temperate highlands and extensive high-altitude plateaus and valleys of its tremendous cordillera, which was many times the number of persons living at that time in Spain. And these tens of millions of natives of the Americas were thoroughly accustomed, by a civilized cultural heritage going back twenty centuries, to being ruled by and paying taxes (tribute) to their native lords. They comprised highly valuable new subjects for the Spanish king if conquered by military forces loyal to him.

There were four of these civilizations which the extraordinary perceptiveness and bravery of Hernan Cortes, Francisco Pizarro, and other valiant Spanish conquistadors subjected to Spanish rule in little more than a couple of decades in the early sixteenth century. The Maya civilization of present-day Guatemala and the Yucatan, which was in decline when it was conquered; the Chibcha civilization in what is now Colombia which gave rise to the legend of "El Dorado" (the man of gold); the Aztec suzerainty in Mexico; and the Inca empire centered in Peru. Nothing like the cities the Spaniards saw in Mexico's Central Valley in the shadows of snow-crowned volcanic peaks or the Inca cities on the *altiplano* of South America existed elsewhere in the Americas. The splendor of these New World civilizations impressed the Spanish conquistadors and increased their ardor to conquer them. The Aztec metropolis of Tenochtitlan (present-day Mexico City), for instance, was larger than any city in sixteenth-century Europe and had a daily market surpassing in its volume and variety of goods for sale the annual fair held at Medina del Campo, Spain, whose fame brought merchants from all over Europe to participate in it. Bernal Diaz del Castillo's *The True History of the Conquest of Mexico* is an eyewitness account, by a conquistador who accompanied Cortes, of the magnificence beheld by the first Spaniards to enter the Valley of Mexico, and Garcilaso de la Vega's *The Royal Commentaries of the Incas* is a similar contemporary report of the grandeur of the Inca imperium. *Daily Life of the Aztecs on the Eve of the Spanish Conquest* by Jacques Soustelle (Stanford University Press, 1961) and Burr Cartwright Brundage's *Lords of Cuzco: A History and Description of the Inca People in Their Final Days* (University of Oklahoma Press, 1967) are scholarly studies of these subjects. Friedrich Katz, *The Ancient American Civilizations* (Praeger Publishers, 1972; trans. K. M. Lois Simpson) is a scholarly overview of the history of pre-Columbian civilization in the Americas.

Spanish military commanders had only to conquer and replace the native lords of these lands to convert them into kingdoms and *capitanias* under Spanish rule.

This civilized mountainous region of the Americas in the 1500s contained populations many times larger than the Neolithic parts of the Americas colonized by Europeans, where no rich, populous cities existed to be conquered and governed. What became Spanish America did not have to be populated and developed to make it valuable as did the Stone Age wildernesses of Brazil, Canada, and the Atlantic Coastal Plain of North America. All that was needed in these civilized parts of the Western Hemisphere was to secure and administer them, thereby putting their extant wealth-producing human and natural resources under Spanish rule, a wealth that included fabulous amounts of gold and silver and millions of productive peasant farmers and skilled artisans.

The intellectual and technological attainments of these

indigenous civilizations of the Americas in medicine, surgery, mathematics, astronomy, calendar making, the engineering of precisely graded channels for the long-distance transportation of huge volumes of water and intricate field-irrigation systems for large-scale agriculture, the building of roads and bridges over precipitous terrain, and the architectural planning and construction of great cities with monumental palaces, temples, and fortifications, put them in the same category with Europe's Bronze Age civilizations. But the religious rituals of the Aztecs, which called for human sacrifices by the tens of thousands were horrendous and highly objectionable not only to the Spaniards but to the peoples the Aztecs subjugated to supply the human sacrifices. It was this barbarism on the part of the Aztecs that gave the small Spanish military force commanded by Hernan Cortes the means to break the power of the Aztecs, whose cruelity made the Totonacs, Tlaxcalans, and other peoples of Mexico side with Cortes and furnish him the manpower and supplies which allowed him to establish the first European foothold on the mainland of the Americas.

Chapter Three

AMERICAN SOCIETY

The four European maritime powers bordering the North Atlantic that created enduring overseas settlements on the mainland of North and South America each faced a particular challenge whose solution affected post-1521 cultural developments in the Western Hemisphere. The Spanish crown's problem was governing the tens of millions of new subjects it acquired when its soldiers conquered the New World civilizations. For Portugal, the smallest in size and population of the maritime powers, the problem was how to muster enough manpower to make the Brazilian wilderness profitable. France, the most populous of these powers, had to balance maintaining its dominance in Europe with the need to create a colonial population in Canada. The English kings wanted to populate the Atlantic Coastal Plain with as many people as possible as soon as possible, and at the least cost to the royal treasury, to convert that wilderness into profitable farmland. The common challenge for all four of these Old World monarchies was how to use the lands that Columbus had made known to Europeans to increase their wealth. Planting colonies that would become independent nations was never their intent.

The Spanish crown reasoned that only immigrants of pure Spanish blood (*sangre pura*) descended from generations of Roman Catholics (*católicos viejos*) should be allowed into Spain's new realms in the Americas. All immigration to Spain's new possessions on the American mainland was, therefore, funneled through one port (Seville) and one government bureau in that port (*la Casa de Contratación*) so it could be controlled. Would-be immigrants to Spanish America had to present to the *Casa de Contratación* in Seville sworn testaments from their parish priests that they were observant Roman Catholics of true Spanish birth and that generations of their forbears had likewise been that. This severe screening of immigrants kept Jews, Moslems, and Protestants from immigrating to Spanish America and assured that Spain's territories in the Americas would acquire an upper class of uniform Spanish stock that could be relied on to hold the Indian masses of Spanish America in permanent servitude.

However, as had always been true in the long history of Europeans conquering and ruling other Europeans, members of the former ruling classes of the conquered civilizations in the Americas were recruited to help administer the lands they and their ancestors had ruled. Intermarriage with the former ruling class was also allowed as part of the pacification, provided the intended spouse became a Roman Catholic. Given the disparity between tens of millions of civilized Indians who had been subjected to Spanish rule and the much smaller population of immigrant Spaniards and their descendants, a good deal of miscegenation both with and without benefit of Christian marriage occurred in colonial Spanish American society from the beginning.

Spaniards born in Spain comprised the highest caste in this society, followed by *hidalgos* of pure Spanish pedigree born in the Americas; then persons of Spanish lineage mixed with Indian blood (especially noble Indian stock); then various mixtures of

Spanish, Indian, and Negro blood. At the bottom of this social pyramid based on birth were a small class of slaves of African origin and the masses of Indian peons, who before the advent of the Spanish conquistadors had long been accustomed to being the lowest class in the societies of their birth.

Portugal, the first European nation to traffic in African slaves on a large scale, drew from its slave-trading stations on the west coast of Africa the needed manpower to develop Brazil. Slavery was the chief social and economic institution throughout the three centuries of Brazil's colonial history and well into its history as an independent nation. Roughly 85 percent of Brazil's population was in that condition of servitude until 1871 when a "freedom of the womb" law went into effect emancipating the newborn children of slave mothers, thus gradually abolishing the all-pervasive institution of slavery. The classic history of slavery in Brazil is Gilberto Freyre's *Casa Grande e senzala* (1933) published in the United States as *The Masters and the Slaves: A Study in the Development of Brazilian Civilization* (Alfred A. Knopf, 1946). The Portuguese crown, too, like the Spanish kings, screened immigrants to Brazil for conformity to Portuguese nationality and the Roman Catholic religion, but less rigorously than the Spanish crown.

Although France had by far the largest population of the four major European powers that established long-lasting colonies on the continents of the Western Hemisphere, it sent the fewest immigrants to its colony. Even tiny Portugal provided more immigrants to Brazil than France permitted to go to Canada. The French crown thought it logical to keep French manpower in France to fight the wars that maintained its supremacy in Europe. Besides, no large French population was needed in Canada. Fish and furs were Canada's profitable products, and Indian trappers kept the French fur brokers at Montreal well supplied with luxurious winter pelts to process and ship back to France, while fishing fleets came seasonally from France to take incredible catches of cod from Canada's rich Atlantic fishing grounds without much need to set foot on Canadian soil. Because of France's numerically restrictive immigration policy, Canada one-and-one-half centuries after its first permanent European settlement had less than 100,000 inhabitants, while the thirteen English-speaking colonies to the south had a population of 2,250,000.[1] Canada was the smallest and slowest-growing European colony on the mainland of the Americas.

Canada's main value to the French crown was as a strategic military base for keeping its great European rival, England, from expanding into the Mississippi Valley. The heights which dominate the St. Lawrence River at Quebec, one thousand miles inland from the Atlantic, were ideal for that purpose. (No other large river in North America emptying into the Atlantic had an east-west orientation deep into the interior of the continent.) Canada's population was designed by the French crown as a matter of policy to meet the minimum needs of supporting the fur trade at Montreal and the forts at Quebec and elsewhere in Canada, which were garrisoned by professional troops rotated in from France. This use of Canada served France well until Britain finally succeeded, in 1759, in conquering the bastion at Quebec and, with its fall, all of Canada the following year. The treaty ceding Canada to Britain was signed in 1763.

Like both the Spanish and Portuguese monarchies, the French crown also screened immigration to Canada to ensure uniformity of religion and nationality. Canada in its century and a half of French rule had not only the smallest and slowest growing, but also the most homogeneous population of any

---

1 *The Columbia History of the World*, eds. John A. Garraty and Peter Gay (Harper & Row, 1972), 674. J. L. Finlay and D. N. Sprague, *The Structure of Canadian History*, second edition (Prentice-Hall Canada, 1979), 63. *The Encyclopedia of Colonial and Revolutionary America*, ed. John Mack Faragher (Da Capo Press, 1996), 200.

mainland European colony in the Americas: a society of just one European nationality (French) and one religion (Roman Catholicism). Canada's culture was consequently so Eurocentric that French Canadians in 1776 rejected American overtures to join their war to separate from British rule. French Canadians apparently preferred dependence on a European monarch (even an English monarch) to independence and the formation of a republican government. After America won its war for independence, Canada's Europe-oriented culture was strengthened by the first non-French, non-Catholic immigration in its history, which doubled its population: tens of thousands of American Loyalists fleeing the republican governments established by the States of the United States of America.

The European colonies on the mainland of the Western Hemisphere that became the United States of America were in comparison to the Spanish, Portuguese, and French colonies exceptional in their basic social characteristics.

American colonial society had, for instance, no huge preponderance of Indians as Spanish American society had. The overwhelming majority of tax-paying inhabitants of Spanish America were civilized Indians, but the colonial society of America had hardly any Indians; and the U. S. constitution written, ratified, and amended in 1787-1791 excluded "Indians not taxed" from representation in the U. S. House of Representatives (Article I, Section 2; Amendment XIV, Section 2). Not until Congress passed the Snyder Act which President Calvin Coolidge signed into law in1924 did all Indians born in the United States become U.S. citizens.

Nor did the American colonies have anywhere near the proportion of slaves out of Africa that Brazilian colonial society had. Instead of the approximately 85 percent slave and 15 percent free proportions of Brazil's population, the slave-to-free ratio during America's history of slavery was the reverse. Roughly 85 percent of America's population was free and 15 percent was in the condition of chattel slavery. Similar to Canada and unlike Brazil and Spanish America, the overwhelming majority of America's colonial society—more than four-fifths of it—was of European stock. But these Europeans were from many nations and religions of Europe rather than one nationality and one religion. From the beginning of America's history as an English colonial territory, any European could immigrate to this part of the Western Hemisphere if they swore allegiance to the king of England. Immigrants to colonial America were *self-selecting, not government-screened.*

Why did English monarchs adopt this permissive immigration policy? Did they have an idea of the purpose of colonies different from the monarchs of Spain, Portugal, and France? No, the English kings shared the concept of colonies expressed by the king of Portugal who called Brazil his milk cow. The kings of England had several reasons for not insisting, as their Spanish, Portuguese, and French counterparts did, that only immigrants who were already their subjects and adherents of their state religion be granted entry to their American colonies. The English crown in not screening immigrants according to nationality and religion wanted to maximize immigration to their colonies (unlike the minimalist immigration policy of France regarding Canada) in order to build up as large a population in them as quickly as possible so the wilderness of the Atlantic Coastal Plain would be converted as rapidly as possible into farmland to create taxable transatlantic commerce. The kings of England wanted a rapidly growing colonial population that would export agricultural produce, lumber, ship spars, and marine stores to England and be a market for English goods.

Permissive, unscreened immigration to these colonies also relieved some of the serious religious tensions within England during the century in which twelve of the thirteen English colonies on the North American mainland were chartered. (Georgia, the thirteenth colony, was chartered in 1732.) The 1600s was a century of extraordinary ongoing political and religious turmoil in England in consequence of the previous century's disestablishment of Roman Catholicism as England's official state religion and the establishment of a new, Protestant religion (the Church of England) instituted by law as the new state religion of English government. Between 1620 and 1690, England experienced recurring political and religious strife, the upheaval of a civil war, the trial and execution of a reigning king, seven years of military dictatorship, the restoration to the throne of a son of the executed king, and finally (in 1688) the offer of the crown to a new royal line (the English princess Mary and her Dutch husband William of Orange) on condition that they and their heirs would be communicants of the Church of England and accept Parliament's constitutional supremacy in England's government.

In the troubled seventeenth century, England's American colonies became a haven for English Catholics and English Protestants such as the Puritans and the Quakers whose religious practices and beliefs did not conform to those of the Church of England and for Protestants who were being persecuted in other parts of Europe. Indeed, Massachusetts, Maryland, Pennsylvania, and Rhode Island were founded by private persons ("proprietors") as asylums for persons fleeing religious persecution, all of them having received authorizing charters from the English crown.

During the colonial period of the 1600s and 1700s—the formative centuries of American culture—non-English immigration to the American colonies of the English crown steadily increased. (One authority on the early history of American demography has estimated that by the time the War for Independence began "roughly half of the inhabitants of the Thirteen

Colonies had no English blood in their veins."[2]) An eighteenth-century French immigrant to America, Michel Guillaume St. John de Crevecoeur, in his book *Letters From An American Farmer* (1782) about his experiences in America in the decades leading up to the War for Independence, emphasized that, "Here individuals of all nations are melted into a new race of men … a new man who acts on new principles." Crevecoeur averred that in America "the name of Englishman, Frenchman, and European is lost" and that from a "mixture of English, Scotch, Irish, French, Dutch, Germans, and Swedes" arises "the race now called Americans." No other place of European settlement in the New World, Crevecoeur said (and he was on the scene and a keen observer), represented such a "strange mixture of blood" from forbears who were "once scattered all over Europe."[3] Thomas Paine, writing from Philadelphia in 1776, said the same thing in his observation that "Europe, and not England, is the parent country of America."[4]

America's population was soley European only from 1607 to 1619. In 1619 a score of free blacks from the Caribbean immigrated to Virginia as indentured servants. John Hope Franklin, the dean of black American historians, in his magisterial work *From Slavery to Freedom*, observed that these twenty black immigrants "were not slaves in a legal sense." They were, Franklin wrote, "simply more indentured servants," and in the next half century before chattel slavery was instituted in Virginia "the records reveal an increasing number of free Negroes" among the influx of immigrants to Virginia.[5]

---

2   Gary B. Nash, *Red, White, and Black: The Peoples of Early America,* second edition (Prentice-Hall, 1982), 200.
3   *Letters From An American Farmer,* eds. Henri L. Bourdin, Ralph H. Gabriel, and Stanley T. Williams (Yale University Press, 1925), 74, 68-70.
4   "Common Sense," *Thomas Paine Reader,* eds. Michael Foot and Isaac Kramnick (Penguin, 1987), 81.
5   John Hope Franklin, *From Slavery to Freedom: A History of Negro Americans,* Fifth Edition (Alfred A. Knopf, 1980), 54-55.

In 1624, the Dutch built a trading post on the Hudson at what is now Albany and two years later a second trading post at the lower end of Manhattan Island. The Dutch were also the first Europeans to settle New Jersey. Swedes and Finns (from whom the building of log cabins derived) were the first European settlers of Pennsylvania and Delaware, decades before William Penn showed up in 1692. The English navy soon subjected these non-English settlements on the Atlantic Coastal Plain to British rule, but their Dutch, Swedish, and Finnish inhabitants were not expelled. They became part of the mix of European nationalities in America that Crevecoeur identified. In addition to all of those nationalities, there were immigrants from at least nine other parts of Europe: Bohemia, Denmark, Flanders, Italy, Poland, Portugal, Spain, Switzerland, and Wales.

The religions of these nationalities were also varied: Baptist, Church of England, Congregationalist, Dutch Reformed, German Reformed, Jewish, Lutheran, Methodist, Moravian, Pietistic, Quaker, Roman Catholic, and Shaker, to mention only some of the multitude of religions in colonial America. The profusion of religious denominations reflects of course the English crown's policy of not requiring adherence to the state religion of England as a qualification for immigrating to these colonies—a condition the Spanish, Portuguese, and French crowns did impose on immigration to their New World colonies. And once again no greater tolerance of religious differences on the part of England's kings explains the policy. The kings of England believed just as strongly as the kings of Spain, Portugal, and France in the principle of one-state, one-religion. But the English government had a problem the other European overseas imperialists did not have: a large number of religious dissidents or "Non-Conformists." America was a dumping ground for alleviating the problem of religious non-conformity in England.

It is indicative of the cultural divergence that had developed between England and America by the eighteenth century that Englishmen sometimes solaced themselves following the War for Independence for their loss of their American colonies by saying Americans were, after all, "a mongrel breed." During that war, Britain won many battles and at various times occupied America's largest cities: Boston, Charleston, Philadelphia (the largest English-speaking city in the world outside London in the eighteenth-century), and New York. But no British army ever cornered an American army in the field and captured it. The "mongrel breed" did that twice: once at Saratoga in 1777 and again at Yorktown in 1781. And the primary reason for those debacles, which caused George III to lose his war to subdue his rebellious subjects in America, may well have been the attitude of Britain's aristocratic generals, who found it impossible to take seriously English-speaking men "without breeding," which led them to disdain and underestimate the military prowess of their ill-bred, "mongrel" opponents.

Government screening of immigrants by nationality and religion replicates in the colony the colonizing country's society as nearly as that can be done. But what effect does self-selected immigration have? What sort of a society is produced when self selecting immigration is allowed? What behavioral characteristics accumulate in a colonial society where self-selected immigrants and their descendants predominate?

Sociologists attribute the phenomenon of immigration to what they call "Push-Pull": the push of conditions in the place of the immigrant's origin and the pull of conditions in the place where he is thinking of going. That is a valid analysis as far as it goes, but it leaves out a crucial factor: temperament. It takes a person with a certain kind of character to abandon everything familiar, perhaps everyone the immigrant loves, and go to a strange, far-off place where those with whom one will be living may not even speak one's language. This is to say that not every hungry Irishman during the Irish potato famine in the 1840s got on a ship bound for America, where food was known to be plentiful. Only Irishmen with a certain kind of temperament and outlook on life did that.

Basically, a self-selecting immigrant is a *self-respecting failure bent on success.* He is someone who feels he is failing to get in his native place the satisfaction from life and wherewithal to live as he feels he should live; he imagines he can find in the place of his contemplated immigration that satisfaction and wherewithal through his own initiative and diligent hard work (hence the self-respecting part of the definition). The self-respecting failure bent on success is moved by his *imagination* of a new life (his vision of a better future, if not for himself then for his offspring); by his *hope* that his change in residence will lead to opportunities for improving his life; and by his *confidence* in his ability to determine his future on his own terms through his own efforts. The self-selecting immigrants who went to America wanted to be free of the socio-economic constraints inherent to societies based on birth-determined classes. They wanted to be self-determining. They were individualists who were willing to live among strangers and compete with them.

Another aspect of their character is also important. They were brave. Landsmen unaccustomed to the sea had to have a good deal of courage to leave the sight of land and go on a long voyage of uncertain duration, living in a cramped compartment aboard a ship crowded with strangers. Only persons who would brave the uncertainty and harsh conditions of such a voyage became immigrants. The dangers inherent to it included gales and monstrous waves which could swamp a wooden ship and send it to the bottom of the North Atlantic, drowning everyone onboard. There was also the danger of pirates. The desperate nausea ("seasickness") caused by the side-to-side and up-and-down motions of a ship at sea was another well-known hazard in the days of wooden sailing vessels sufficient to deter even intrepid would-be immigrants. There was also the risk of hunger if the voyage was unduly prolonged by adverse winds or an absence of wind. For in the days of the wooden sailing ships, passengers provided their own provisions, and transatlantic crossings lasting a lot longer than the normal six to ten weeks could mean starvation if food and water ran out. (One hundred and forty-four Englishmen left London in 1606, for instance, to establish the colony in Virginia, but only 105 survived the voyage, which lasted more than twice the time of a normal transatlantic crossing: a death toll of 27 percent.) A death rate of 10 percent was common from the serious illnesses bred in the dank, crowded, unsanitary compartments of the wooden immigrant ships during the seventeenth and eighteenth centuries, the formative centuries of American culture. Children and the elderly were the most susceptible to the shipboard diseases that caused so many immigrants to be buried at sea. (Of course the gift of imagination that was one of the distinguished traits of the self-selected immigrants magnified all of these risks.) Francis Scott Key's poem of 1814 which provided the lyrics for "The Star-Spangled Banner" in referring to America as "the home of the brave" was not exaggerating.

No matter what part of the world the immigrants came from or the century in which they came or what their language, religion or social class was, the seaborne immigrants to America had more in common with each other than they did with those they left behind in their respective countries. It required certain traits to board the ships for America: hope, initiative, self-confidence, bravery, and a daring imagination. The process of self-selection made these Europeans *proto-Americans*. The women among them in their bravery, imaginativeness, and determination to succeed also fit the prototype as much as the men. This is to say that the self-selecting immigrants had traits of character not commonly found in their stay-at-home peers left behind in "the Old Country" on the other side of "the Pond," as the immigrants and their offspring in America deprecatingly referred to the Atlantic once that formidable barrier had been safely crossed. They did, indeed, as Crevecoeur said, act on "new principles." Each of them in going to America was working a revolution in his or her life, and once a functioning society of such persons and their descendants (who acquired their parents' beliefs through imitating their behavior) accumulated in America and began acting generation after generation in non-European ways a new set of cultural beliefs, revolutionarily different from the culture of Europe, began to form in what was to become, in 1776, the United States of America.

The government-screened immigrants to Spanish America and Brazil had a different expectation and character. Simply by going to Spanish America or Brazil, they knew they would be moving up in social rank to become part of the upper class in those colonies. There was no uncertainty about that. They would by blood and baptism be members of the class which ruled the Indian masses in Spanish America or the masses of Negro slaves in Brazil, no matter what their personal merits might be or what their social status in Spain or Portugal had been. Moreover, these government-screened immigrants knew that the societies in Spanish America and Brazil they would be joining would have the same structure of birth-classes they were accustomed to in Europe and the same state religion and language as their homeland. Nothing in the society they would be entering would be altogether new except the climate and topography.

For the government-screened immigrants who crossed the Atlantic to Canada, there was no automatic promotion into a ruling class, since no non-French, servile majority existed in Canada for an immigrant from France to be automatically superior to. The government-screened immigrants to Canada were simply going to a miniature, more homogeneous version of their homeland with a much colder climate. They would retain the same class status they had had in France. But because Canadian society was much smaller, there might be greater opportunity for advancement there than in France. *Peut-être.* However, the same necessity of finding favor through some well-bred patron would apply with the same cultural rigor in Canada as it did in France.

The self-selected immigrants who went to America were leaving behind the aristocratic societies of Europe and plunging into a quite different sort of society: a free-for-all in which everyone's social status was up for grabs and would be decided mainly by the hurly-burly of individual effort and personal success rather than by European-style patronage. Charles Pinckney (1757-1824), who fought in the War for Independence and was a leading delegate to the Constitutional Convention, a four-term governor of his home State (South Carolina), a U.S. Senator, and American ambassador to Spain, put the difference between European and American culture this way:

> We have been taught here to believe that all power of right belongs to the people; that it flows immediately from them, and is delegated to their officers for the public good; that our rulers are the servants of the people, amenable to their will, and created for their use. How different are the governments of Europe! There, the people are the servants and subjects of the rulers; there, merit and talents have little or no influence; but all the honors and offices of government are swallowed up by birth, by fortune, or by rank. From the European world are no precedents to be drawn for a people who think they are capable of governing themselves.[6]

The nature of American society resulted primarily from the

---

6 Quoted in W. Cleon Skousen, *The Making of America: The Substance and Meaning of the Constitution* (National Center for Constitutional Studies, 1985), 168-69.

character of the self-selected immigrant and secondarily from their origin in a multitude of European nationalities and religions.

The chief characteristic of self-selected immigrants was their desire to "get ahead," to improve their lives, and to be free and self-determining. They were ambitious to achieve a level of property ownership that would make them and their offspring independent. They did not want to be beholden, as people generally were in Europe, to men of "noble blood" who monopolized the upper ranks of society and perpetuated their alleged superiority through the privileges of their birth and by dispensing patronage. The self-selected immigrant in leaving Europe for America was choosing to leave that kind of society behind. There were no "noblemen" in America. Achievement, not birth, is what mattered in American society. Never before had there been a society overwhelmingly composed of individuals who had or whose ancestors had *chosen* to belong to it. American society was not composed of birth classes but of self-determining individualists seeking success. This society was exceptional. Its character was basically non-European in nature.

The first thing about this way of life that distinguished it from the culture of Europe concerned work. In America, everyone had to work. With a wilderness to be converted into farms and towns, there could be no tolerance for a class of people who did not work. In England, the point of being in the upper class was to be exempt from labor and to lead a leisured life. One's position in England's upper class was attained by birth and inheritance; whatever else that might mean, it meant you performed no manual labor. The purpose of being of the "genteel" class was to be waited upon hand and foot. To belong to the upper class meant enjoying a social status that entailed not getting your hands dirty, which in Europe was an indication of membership in an inferior class. In America that was not the case. There, manual work was the ordinary means of acquiring property and thus comfort and respectability. Contrary to the European way of life, manual labor in America carried no stigma of social inferiority. Historically, American society has been a society of ambitious individuals who derived their self-respect from their work. The importance of work in American culture is reflected in what Americans typically want to know on first acquaintance with a stranger: "What do you do?" and by Americans taking far fewer holidays from work than Europeans do.

The founding of Jamestown illustrates this cultural divide regarding work. Jamestown was top-heavy with gentlemen. Only twelve of its original 105 settlers were on the company's rolls as "Laborers." The designation undoubtedly meant a worker of no particular skill because another twelve persons were identified as having a noteworthy skill: four carpenters, a barber, a black-smith, a bricklayer, a drummer, a mason, a sailor, a surgeon, and a tailor. These twenty-four men were the colony's workforce. The other eighty-one males who went ashore at Jamestown in 1607 (there were no women in the company) were identified on the colony's rolls as "Gentlemen" (fifty-four persons) or "Boys" and "diverse others" (twenty-seven), who were almost certainly the body servants of the gentlemen. This 3:1 ratio of gentlemen and their servants to workers to fell trees, build huts, clear fields, plant crops, erect a palisade to protect the settlement, or per-form some other manual labor for the good of the community was a serious problem.

English gentlemen were culturally accustomed to having their sustenance provided to them without any physical labor on their part to produce it. They were used to inheriting their housing. But in a wilderness, where is sustenance and shelter to come from for persons who will not work? In making a settle-ment in a wilderness, the necessity of work is fundamental and unremitting. There is not time to be both a body servant to a gentleman and a laborer doing the needed heavy work in such a place.

With few exceptions, the only work most of the English gentlemen at Jamestown, who made up a little over half of the colonists, were willing to perform was the search for gold. And they actually found enough of the gold-colored, glittering pyrite called "Fool's Gold" to load a ship with it and send it off to London for assay, contrary to the advice of their peers at Jamestown who sensibly pointed out that if gold existed in this part of the New World, the natives would long since have found it. But the Virginia tribes wore no ornaments of gold. Only the willingness of some of the fifty-four gentlemen at Jamestown to put aside their cultural dignity and get their hands dirty in the heavy labor of felling trees, making crops, and performing the other necessary manual labors of a colony being hewn out of a wilderness offered the struggling little settlement on the Virginia coast any prospect of survival and possible future prosperity.

The famous Captain John Smith was one of these adaptable gentlemen; in a letter he wrote to the colony's backers in London, he complained about the "slothful and idle drones" who were consuming Jamestown's limited supplies of food without doing anything to augment them. He told Jamestown's backers in London (for Jamestown was the enterprise of a joint-stock company which hoped to turn a profit from its investment) that he would sooner see "thirty Carpenters, husbandmen, gardeners, fisher men, blacksmiths, masons, and diggers up of trees" landed in Virginia than a thousand lay-about gentlemen. In the book of instructions for founders of colonies Smith subsequently wrote based on his experiences in America, he emphasized that no one who could not "well brook labour" should be permitted to immigrate to a colony planted in a wilderness. The success of such a colony, he wrote, depended on never allowing "Masters, Gentlemen, Gentlewomen, and children" who would not perform manual labor to outnumber "men to work,"[7] as had happened at Jamestown.

Those who remained in England did not understand the need in America for non-European cultural behaviors about class and work. Cultures resist change even in the face of demanding realities, as can be seen in the *Fundamental Constitutions of Carolina*. In the 1660s, England's king gave eight high-ranking Englishmen title to what is now the States of North and South Carolina, and they assigned the task of creating a plan for governing this immense grant of land to the English political philosopher John Locke. The plan Locke drew up in 1669 (the *Fundamental Constitutions of Carolina*) called for most of the territory to be distributed to titled noblemen whose lands and political authority were to be hereditary. Naturally, at the apex of this social hierarchy were the eight high-ranking English gentlemen, each of whom was to have the title "Lord Proprietor" and 12,000 acres in every county to be surveyed from the territory the king had given them, whose total extent was greater than England's. Below these "Lord Proprietors" came, in order of their holdings in land: "Barons," "Landgraves," "Caciques," and "Lords of Manors." Such titles avoided conflict with England's long-established titles of Marquis, Count, Duke, and Earl; the title "Baron" provided some continuity with England. Persons owning fifty acres were to be allowed to vote, but holding public office was reserved for the projected ruling class of noblemen. The plan's flaw was the extreme cheapness of land in the Carolinas. Even as late as 1750, a square mile of it could be bought for just three shillings, the cost of half a gallon of whiskey.[8]

The *Fundamental Constitutions* was obviously an attempt to

---

7 Smith, *Travels II*, 390, 516, and Smith, *Advertisements for the Unexperienced Planters of New England, or Anywhere: or, The Pathway to Erect a Plantation* (William Veazie, 1865; first published in 1631), 15-16, 40-41.

8 John Mack Faragher, *Daniel Boone: The Life and Legend of an American Pioneer* (Henry Holt, 1992), 29, 40.

replicate English society in the wilds of America. It didn't work. Too much undeveloped land was available in America for next to nothing (or for nothing simply by "squatting" on it) to permit divvying up the Carolinas as England had been among the Duke of Normandy's vassals after his conquest of it in 1066. Individual, land-hungry immigrants were constantly invading the Carolinas to take up land in whatever amounts they could handle and afford and, later on, acquiring as much more land as their circumstances permitted. The same thing was happening in all of the colonies chartered by the English crown on the coastal plain of eastern North America. Moreover, none of the eight Lord Proprietors who paid John Locke to draw up a plan for the Carolinas wanted to leave England to live in an incipient society being hacked from a wilderness. To leave the familiar luxury they were accustomed to in England was too much to ask of them and their ladies. Nor could a sufficient number of other well-bred Englishmen be talked into going to the Carolinas to live and take up the political responsibilities of the lesser nobility that Locke's plan called for. The *Fundamental Constitutions* was unsuited to what was happening in America. It was out of touch with the realities of life as it had to be lived in America.

Never in English society had so large a proportion of "commoners" become freeholders as became owners of small parcels of land in America. For instance in 1764, the governor of Massachusetts reported that less than 2 percent of the farmers in that colony were renting the land they tilled; the other 98 percent were owners. What was said of seventeenth-century colonial Virginia, that "the small landholder constituted the major group,"[9] was generally true in all the English colonies facing the Atlantic, where impoverished but hardworking immigrants from at least nineteen European nationalities were able to purchase land if they

---

9 W. Stitt Robinson, Jr., *Mother Earth: Land Grants in Virginia 1607-1699* (Virginia 350th Anniversary Celebration Corporation, 1957), 74.

worked diligently and were frugal, because wages for hired labor in America were much higher than in Europe due to its comparative scarcity, cheap land was readily available, and taxes were much less. (Laborers in America in the late 1700s earned fifteen times more than the yearly income of two pounds that defined an English yeoman.[10]) In 1813, Thomas Jefferson said of America that "every one may have land to labor for himself, if he chuses; or, preferring the exercise of any other industry, may exact for it such compensation as not only to afford a comfortable subsistence, but wherewith to provide for a cessation from labor in old age."[11]

Because land in America was cheap and plentiful while labor for hire was scarce and costly, property owners looked for ways to obtain cheap labor. The first institution to serve this need was devised in the first few years of Virginia's history: indentured servitude. This was a form of temporary slavery. A person who wanted to go to America to improve his lot in life but could not afford the price of the passage signed a contract or "indenture," agreeing to work a specified number of years (the average was four years[12]) for room and board but no wages in exchange for having his passage to America taken care of. Ship captains in the seventeenth and eighteenth centuries made a regular business of signing up indentured workers in Europe, carrying them across the Atlantic, and selling their contracts to American property owners. More than half (perhaps as many as three-quarters) of the immigrants during the colonial era came to America in the condition of indentured servitude. To further alleviate the scarcity of labor for hire in America, a comparatively small portion of the immigration from England were convicts who had committed relatively minor offenses and were sentenced to work off the term of their

10 Thomas Fleming, "America 1776," *Reader's Digest* (July 1976), 55; Clarence L. Ver Steeg, *The Formative Years 1607-1763* (Hill and Wang, 1964), 66.
11 Jefferson to John Adams, October 28, 1813, *Jefferson Writings*, 1309.
12 *Encyclopedia of American History, Bicentennial Edition*, ed. Richard B. Morris (Harper & Row, 1976), 160.

punishment in America. Some orphans were also forced to go to America as bound apprentices. The practice of indentured servitude continued in America through the early 1800s.

The other institution created for the purpose of providing cheap labor was of even more benefit to property owners. Chattel slavery became lawful in Virginia in the 1660s and spread north and south from there and lasted until 1865. The sinful allure of chattel slavery was that for a large initial outlay of money to purchase the body of a slave, the slave owner obtained for himself without further expense except food, lodging, and clothing for the slave, a lifetime of labor, and in the case of a female slave, the investment additionally bought a lifetime of labor from the children she might bear or the profit of selling them as commodities on the slave market.

Laborers for hire in America found (as Jefferson reported) that they could command high wages, and many who were diligent in putting aside some of their earnings found themselves in a few years able to purchase property and thereby leave the pool of workers for hire. And of course in many instances, these former hired laborers who became property owners wanted hired help to improve their property and make it more profitable. The chance for social advancement that attracted impoverished European immigrants to America and allowed many of them to become property owners thus led to the institution of chattel slavery, which denied freedom and opportunity to enslaved Africans and put them in the inhuman condition of being live or chattel property, the same legal category as livestock.

The year following the end of the War for Independence, Benjamin Franklin characterized America as a "Land of Labour."[13] But the working poor of England had long referred to America as "the best poor man's country," and from letters

---

13 "Information to Those Who Would Remove to America" (1784), *Benjamin Franklin Writings*, 978.

written home by immigrants who had succeeded in America, the poor and middle classes in many countries of Europe acquired a knowledge of the opportunities for employment available there and America's comparatively high wages, cheaper prices, and lower taxes.

The per capita wealth of America in the eighteenth century was higher than that of England,[14] though of course colonial America's total wealth was still well below the accumulated wealth of England's many-centuries-old, aristocratic society. Longevity—another index of a society's prosperity besides per capita wealth—was also exceptional in America. The natural supply of wild meat and fish and the abundance of cultivated food available through America's proliferating family farms caused Americans on average to be better nourished and to live longer than the average European in the seventeenth and eighteenth centuries. Not until the 1890s, for example, did England achieve the low infant mortality rate and longevity New England had in the 1600s.[15]

To civilize *in less than three centuries* a Stone Age wilderness that was the entire middle portion of the world's third-largest continent (the U. S. Census Bureau reported in 1890 that the density of population throughout the contiguous United States was greater than that which defines a frontier) required exceptional initiative and a cultural dedication to hard work. There was, of course, a connection between such comparatively swift continental development and the extraordinary volume of immigration to America. The connection was the opportunities for immigrants and their descendants who had the imagination to see them and the willingness to make the most of them.

The central portion of North America from ocean to ocean, as noted before, presented the only continent-size temperate

---

14 James T. Lemon, *The Best Poor Man's Country* (Norton, 1976), 229, note 1.
15 T. H. Hollingsworth, *Historical Demography* (Cornell University Press, 1969), 179.

zone in the Western Hemisphere having a lot of arable land. It was also the only part of the Western Hemisphere during the era of European colonization that had an open immigration policy regarding nationality and religion. By leaving for America, the most enterprising of Europe's lower and middling classes could escape the restraints of societies based on birth classes. The exceptional opportunities that America offered attracted a unique society of workers focused on improving their social status, a society that by the mid-eighteenth century had become the world's most innovative, dynamic, and individualistic society.

But if American society has historically been an accumulation of self-reliant go-getters, how is it that American culture produced such a strong belief in helping others, which expresses itself in behaviors ranging from simple person-to-person neighborliness toward strangers to numerous multi-million-dollar institutions of philanthropy? (In the decade 1985-1995, for instance, the annual charitable donations of individual Americans averaged $89 billion and U.S. corporations and foundations contributed another $20 billion on average each year of that decade, while in 1996 charitable donations by individuals in America reached a whopping $150.7 billion.[16]) If a monetary value is assigned the charitable volunteer work that roughly half the U.S. population eighteen and older performs annually, the value of individual giving in the United States is much higher. Why do Americans on average contribute more of their time and money to charitable endeavors than any other people on earth? What connection is there between American culture and the extraordinary level of charitable giving by Americans?

The connection is self-interest. Benjamin Franklin (1706-1790) understood that improving a community improves the lives of every member of the community including the one who

---

16 *World Almanac and Book of Facts 1997*, 713. Susan Jacoby, "Why Do We Donate? It's Personal," *New York Times*, December 9, 1997, G1.

encourages and organizes the funding of the improvements. In his *Autobiography*, which has never been out of print since it was first published, Franklin often expounds on this idea of enlightened self-interest, which led him to become America's first fundraiser for community improvements (street-cleaning, a hospital, a lending library, etc.) and to come up with the idea of "matching funds." Franklin knew how to appeal to the competitiveness of Americans and made fundraising a contest to match or surpass another person's public-spirited generosity. His ingenuity and interest in improvements also led him to come up with the idea of daylight savings time to give workers in his day who labored from dawn to dark some free hours of daylight during the summer months.

The lesson of enlightened self-interest was learned on the American frontier. People on a thinly populated frontier had to take an interest in each other's welfare and to help one another if they were to survive and prosper. The good of the community was in the best interest of its individual members. That was the lesson the American frontier taught in no uncertain terms. Anyone brought up in a farming district or small town in the United States has experienced the neighborliness of such places. But charity and cooperation—enlightened self-interest—is not restricted to small-town rural America. It exists also in America's cities, because belief-behaviors growing out of the experience of the American frontier became a part of American culture and influenced every community in America, whether rural or urban. The centuries-long process of civilizing a continental expanse of Stone Age wilderness was the most influential event in America's cultural history.

Benjamin Franklin's life illustrates many of the belief-behaviors of American culture. His focus on success and the future and his civic mindedness and leadership led to his rise from a printer's apprentice and self-educated writer to wealth and reputation in

Philadelphia and then renown throughout America as publisher of the popular *Poor Richard's Almanac* and postmaster for the thirteen colonies. Then he retired from business and politics and devoted himself to basic scientific research into the mysteries of electricity and made some of the fundamental discoveries about its nature (negative and positive charges, for instance) for which England's and Scotland's oldest universities awarded him honorary doctorate degrees and learned societies on the Continent, as well as in England, extended membership to him. In the last decades of his long life, Dr. Franklin added to his accomplishments those of a world-class diplomat and one of the founders of the American republic. He was a leading member of the thirty-nine pragmatic patriots who wrote and signed the Constitution of the United States to "secure the Blessings of Liberty to ourselves and our Posterity."

Franklin's varied accomplishments represent a superlative fulfillment of the success self-selected immigrants dreamed of for themselves or their offspring (his immigrant father and a paternal uncle were from a middling family of English freeholders and Non-Conformists). Franklin's talent for organizing socially useful institutions (several of which still exist because of their usefulness), along with his invention of the lightening rod, the Franklin Stove, and bifocal eyeglasses, made him the most prominent genius in early America. As a quintessential American, he was interested in improvements not just for his own benefit but for the benefit of future generations of Americans. (He never patented his inventions, saying he had benefited from those of his predecessors.) Franklin's future orientation, his inventiveness and keen interest in practical social improvements, his go-ahead self-confidence, his organizational skills, amiability, charitableness, and ambition ("An empty sack cannot stand upright") reflect deeply-held beliefs and basic traits of the national character.

While Franklin's genius as an inventor of concepts, things, and organizations may have been extraordinary, Alexis de Tocqueville, who published in 1835 *Democracy in America,* an insightful view of American culture by an admiring upper-class European, saw the impulse to organize as an American social trait. "Americans of all ages, all conditions, and all dispositions constantly form associations," he wrote.[17] As indeed they most certainly do. By the time Franklin began his civic improvements in Philadelphia in the 1700s, there were already in America "numerous voluntary organizations."[18] This pronounced tendency of Americans to form an association to meet some need—whereas in Europe, Tocqueville noted, the government or a titled nobleman would be expected to take the lead—has attained such astonishing proportions in the United States that numerous associations have been formed to serve clusters of related associations, for example (to name only a few): the American Public Transit Association (1,100 organizations), the National Council of Women of the United States (an affiliation of national organizations devoted to women's interests), the U.S. Golf Association (8,600 clubs), the Council of Jewish Federations, the American Council of Learned Societies, the National Federation of State High School Associations, the Child Welfare League of America (88 agencies), the National Garden Clubs, Inc., the Amateur Baseball Congress (1,300 leagues), the United States Cerebral Palsy Associations, the Special Libraries Association, etc. Associations to promote individual well-being and social improvements reflect the frontier need for community cooperation for the good of everyone as well as the self-selected immigrant's interest in improving his own life, which he knew would be served

---

17 *Democracy in America,* trans. Henry Reeve, eds. Francis Bowen and Phillips Bradley (Knopf, 1945), 2 vols., II, I 06.

18 James Truslow Adams, *Provincial Society, 1690-1763* (Macmillan, 1928), 260-64.

through institutionalized efforts to improve society as a whole, in addition to his striving to improve his individual life.

Another aspect of the constant striving of self-selected immigrants and their descendants for improvement was the connection they made between success and movement, which originated in the move of self-selected immigrants to America in quest of success. Early in U. S. history, Americans dug a canal across the neck of land separating the Chesapeake from the lower reaches of the Delaware River in order to speed up the movement of people and goods between Baltimore, Philadelphia, and New York and make the transportation cheaper. By 1825, a 40-foot wide canal for barges had been dug across the length of the State of New York (363 miles with a vertical lift of 571 feet) to connect four of the five sea-like Great Lakes in the upper Midwest with the Atlantic by way of the Hudson River and the port of New York. Also in the early 1800s a series of north-south canals were constructed to connect those same immense lakes to navigable tributaries of the Ohio and Mississippi to move goods and people between the Great Lakes and the Gulf of Mexico and to make transportation by water possible between them and much of the upper Great Plains via the Missouri and its tributaries.

The Mississippi and its two biggest tributaries, the Missouri and the Ohio, comprise nearly 6,000 miles of waterways. Other principal navigable tributaries—the Allegheny, Arkansas, Cumberland, Illinois, James, Little Missouri, Osage, Platte, Red, Republican, St. Francis, Tennessee, Wabash, White, Wisconsin, and Yellowstone rivers—added 16,000 miles to the network of rivers in the center of the country for transporting people and goods by barge, scow, and shallow-draft steamboat. The development of man-made and natural waterways required the kind of imagination and interest in movement manifested in the basic character of the self-selected immigrants.

Americans also demonstrated an early attention to overland transportation. Daniel Boone in 1775 blazed a horse trail through a "gap" (pass) in the Appalachian Mountains into Kentucky. By 1792, this trail had been improved to a wagon road that carried much of the early migration through the Cumberland Gap into the interior of America. By 1818, a second wagon road, this one paved with crushed stone, had been made farther north to link the headwaters of the Potomac to the headwaters of the Ohio. This "National Road" was soon extended through Ohio, Indiana, and Illinois to the east bank of the Mississippi, opposite St. Louis, Missouri. By 1832, pioneers were migrating by wagon all the way to the Pacific Northwest using a "road" which started in Missouri, traversed the Great Plains, passed through the northern Rocky Mountains, and terminated near the mouth of the Columbia River (the Oregon Trail). By 1855, American engineers had bridged the Mississippi and fourteen years later, in 1869, completed the world's first transcontinental railroad, which joined the already-built railroads of the eastern United States with the Pacific Coast. By the end of the nineteenth century, Americans had laid more miles of track than all of the other principal railroad-building nations of the world (France, Germany, Russia, and Great Britain, including British India) combined. Americans likewise took a leading interest in the nineteenth century in the invention and building of telegraph and telephone systems.

In the early decades of the twentieth century, the world's first factory assembly line for the mass production of automobiles was in operation in the United States and enough dealerships for selling automobiles and enough connected paved roads, repair garages, and facilities for producing and distributing gasoline had been created to make widespread automobile travel in America possible: a mode of transportation perfectly suited to individual freedom of movement. The United States now has more miles of paved roads—over three million—and more motor vehicles than any other nation.

Americans (along with Brazilians) also pioneered the development of airplane travel. Americans have likewise been in the forefront of developing personal computers and other electronic devices to create instant, individual access to a worldwide web of information as well as other applications of convenient personalized communication.

Making improvements in transportation and communications are as culturally embedded in the American way of life as competition, innovation, enlightened self-interest, free association, charity, and ambition. America's culture was fundamental to making the first human being to set foot on the moon on July 20, 1969 an American.

All of these developments and America's extraordinarily productive, world leading, free-enterprise economy are connected to the can-do, future-oriented, hardworking, hopeful, improvement-seeking, imaginative character of the self-selecting immigrants and their descendants and the culture they created.

Chapter Four

AMERICAN GOVERNMENT

Under England's so-called "unwritten constitution" (the accumulation of laws concerning how the realm was to be governed which started with Magna Carta in 1215), the crown bore primary responsibility for colonies. The political turmoil afflicting the crown during the 1600s allowed England's colonies on the Atlantic seaboard of North America more freedom of action than they would otherwise have enjoyed if the English kings had not been so distracted during that initial part of America's cultural history. The resulting "salutary neglect" (as it has been termed) contributed to the comparatively rapid development of a sense of independence among these colonists. But the principal factor in that development was the crown's decision to administer its North American colonies at the least possible expense to the royal treasury.

To lessen administrative expenses to the crown, the charters the English kings issued to create their colonies on the coastal plain of North America stipulated that the colonists were to bear the cost of their defense. Unlike the kings of Spain, Portugal, and France, the English kings furnished neither troops nor funds to defend their colonies, though the English Royal Navy patrolled their coasts. Indeed, the kings of England called upon their North American subjects to contribute troops for England's four wars with France in the seventeenth and eighteenth centuries, during which wars all-American forces conquered some French strongholds, most notably Louisburg in 1745, Canada's second-largest fortification. American militia also played a major role in Britain's failed attempt in 1741 to capture Cartagena, the principal bastion of Spain on the mainland of South America, where they were ordered to take the strategic heights above the fortress, which they did, though few survived the assault. By the time the War for Independence began, Americans had a long tradition of battlefield valor and of planning and carrying out military campaigns adapted to American terrain, though they had neither Britain's professional army nor its cumulative wealth. (The all-day, running battle on April 19, 1775 that began the War for Independence reflects American military capabilities: 90 American militia dead and wounded, compared to 269 casualties for the British regulars; the second, larger battle two months later outside Boston showed similar results: 441 American casualties to British losses of 1,150.[1])

Some of the charters the kings of England issued to their North American colonies were to corporations, others were grants to individual proprietors, and a few were for colonies under direct royal control. But regardless of the type of charter that was given, they all required the colonists to pay the cost of the colony's military defense and the salaries of the governors that would be appointed to head their governments. The charters the crown issued to their North American colonies therefore authorized the election of colonial "assemblies" or legislatures to levy taxes to cover these expenses. The first elected assembly having the power to tax was Virginia's House of Burgesses, which

---

1   Mark Mayo Boatner III, *Encyclopedia of the American Revolution, Bicentennial Edition* (David McKay, 1976), 631, 129.

met just twelve years after the first permanent English settlement on the North American mainland was planted at Jamestown in 1607. No other European colonies in the Western Hemisphere had from their imperial masters in Europe the power to tax and directly defray the costs of their governments and to recruit, pay for, and equip militias and commission all of the officers to command them.

In the vast territory of mainland Spanish America, government power was vested in a pair of *virreyes* (viceroys) seated in the capital cities of Spain's two *reinos* (kingdoms) in the New World: the kingdom of New Spain (Mexico) and the kingdom of Peru. These viceroys represented in the elite "Life Guards" that protected them and the other royal Spanish troops they commanded, and in the splendor of their court life and the opulent palaces they occupied in Mexico City and Lima, the person of the absent king in Madrid. The government structure of colonial Brazil was similarly concentrated in viceregal plenary power. But because Brazil was much smaller than Spanish America, only one viceroy was required there. The government of French Canada was even more Eurocentric and absolutist, because almost half its history coincided with the 72-year reign of the most absolute monarch of post-Renaissance Western Europe: Louis the Fourteenth, who ruled France and its colonies from 1643 to 1715. Only in the English colonies was government—in the interest of sparing the crown expense—dispersed among thirteen elected tax-levying legislatures who paid the salaries of the thirteen colonial governors appointed over them, an arrangement which gave American colonists a good deal of sway over their governors since each of them was beholden for his salary to the people he governed.

The charters the English crown issued specified, however, that no colony could enact a law that conflicted with an English law; and the crown vetted the laws passed by the colonial assemblies to discover and void any that were in conflict with English law. Through this absolute royal veto over colonial legislation, which under England's constitution no higher government power could override, the English crown maintained control over its colonies on the western verge of the Atlantic. Reciprocally—and this understanding of their thirteen charters was extremely important to Americans—the colonists believed the king had no authority to make a law on his own without their consent that they would be compelled to obey.

Gradually, during the course of the seventeenth and eighteen centuries, the crown eliminated corporate colonies and two of the four proprietary colonies and made eleven of the thirteen English-speaking colonies on the mainland of North America royal colonies. By 1752, only Pennsylvania and Maryland had governors not appointed by the crown. In taking over eleven of the English colonies by the middle of the eighteenth century, the crown set the stage for the sort of control the kings of Spain, Portugal, and France had always exerted. But by 1752, the English-speaking colonists on the Atlantic Coastal Plain of North America had through self-taxation been paying for their government and frontier defenses, manning their militias and commissioning the officers who commanded them, for more than seven generations. Therefore, when the Earl who headed the king's advisory council in 1757 announced, in a face-to-face meeting in London with a representative of the American colonies, that "THE KING IS LEGISLATOR OF THE COLONIES," that assertion caused great consternation among the colonists, who regarded it as "new Doctrine" and an arbitrary, illicit alteration of their charters. This momentous confrontation was between the First Earl of Granville, the head of the king's Privy Council, and Benjamin Franklin, who had just arrived in London as agent for the Pennsylvania Assembly and was summoned to the home of Lord Granville, who wanted to communicate to the colonists through Franklin this major change in colonial policy.[2] When they got this news from Franklin, the king's American subjects vehemently resisted the new policy by which the king claimed to have unilateral authority to make laws for his colonial subjects in America, which the colonists saw as a violation of the charters the crown had issued to their ancestors.

Faced with determined resistance, the king retracted his claim. However, Parliament then asserted that it could tax the colonies without their consent and proceeded to do so for the purpose of raising money from them to defray the cost of the recently concluded war of conquest in Canada and to pay for the necessary stationing of garrison troops in Canada to secure the conquest: a war in which Americans had fought at their own expense and the sacrifice of American lives. The Sugar Act of 1764 was the first of these unprecedented parliamentary taxation bills on the colonies. Others like it to the same effect (most notably the Stamp Act) soon followed. They were all vigorously denounced in the colonies and prompted the election of the First Continental Congress to speak and act on behalf of all thirteen American colonies. Boycotts of imported English goods followed, along with local violent protests. British merchants, who were losing transatlantic trade and feared more losses should the attempt to tax the colonies continue, also voiced their opposition to these acts of Parliament and all but one of the parliamentary imposed taxes on the colonies were withdrawn.

But Parliament insisted on keeping the tax on tea to demonstrate its contention that it had a constitutional right and power to tax the colonists without their consent if it chose to do so. After all, some of the king's subjects in Britain had no elected representatives in Parliament yet nonetheless paid taxes. Why should the Americans be any different? To make its understanding of

---

2 *Benjamin Franklin Writings*, 1465-66.

England's constitution quite clear to Americans, Parliament passed on March 11, 1766 "An Act for the better securing the dependence of his Majesty's dominions in America upon the crown and the parliament of Great Britain" (commonly known as the Declaratory Act) which proclaimed:

> ... the said colonies and plantations in *America* have been, are, and of right ought to be, subordinate unto, and dependent upon the imperial crown and parliament of *Great Britain*; and the King's majesty, by and with the advice and consent of the lords spiritual and temporal, and commons of *Great Britain,* in parliament assembled, had, hath, and of right ought to have, full power and authority to make laws and statutes of sufficient force and authority to bind the colonies and people of *America,* subjects of the crown of *Great Britain,* in all cases whatsoever.

Ten years later, in 1776, Thomas Jefferson used some of this wording in the Declaration of Independence's proclamation that the United States of America "are, and of Right ought to be, FREE AND INDEPENDENT STATES" with "full Power" to do everything that independent nations can do, and that all ties to the government of Britain were in all cases whatsoever completely severed.

America's victory in the War for Independence settled the issue of who was and ought to be America's sovereign lawmaker. It was not the king and the colonists acting in concert, as the colonial charters appeared to say; nor was it the king acting alone when it suited his purposes, as he tried to claim in 1757; nor did Parliament have ultimate authority in all cases whatsoever. Rather, the sovereign power in the United States was *the people of the States* acting through their elected representatives in their State legislatures (as they had partly done before 1775 as colonies under the authority of the king and after 1776 as completely independent States) and in a general government for all the States: in both instances under written constitutions that had been approved by representatives chosen by the people of the States. The people of these thirteen colonies had exercised too many self-governing powers for too many generations to allow the king or Parliament to dictate their laws or unilaterally amend their charters for government, as they had attempted to do in 1757-1775, without a parting of the ways. The people of the States were willing to fight an eight-year war with one of Europe's great powers to establish their sovereignty.

Power is the ability to make decisions and have them obeyed. In America that power lies in the will of the people of the States acting through their chosen representatives under the eternal *Laws of Nature and of Nature's God,* as the Declaration of Independence says and as the State constitutions and the Constitution of the United States attest. The peoples' constitutionally elected and appointed representatives exercise legitimate power as long as they obey the will of the people of the States embodied in the State constitutions and the constitution for general government which the people of the States have consented to live under. Of these constitutions, the Constitution of the United States is "the supreme Law of the Land" (Article VI, clause 2), because the people of the States have given it that authority through their sovereign ratification. Therefore, when any representative in a State government or in the general government ignores a requirement of a constitution the people of the States have authorized, they are usurping the people's sovereignty and must be removed from office for that high crime.

The first constitution for general government in the United States (the Articles of Confederation and Perpetual Union) was completed a week after the Declaration of Independence but not ratified for five years because Maryland objected to one of its provisions. Wartime expedience produced the Articles of Confederation, which was largely the work of the man the Second Continental Congress assigned to the task: John Dickinson (1732-1808). Fighting a common enemy held the country together. But six years after the Articles of Confederation were ratified in 1781, it had become clear the Articles were an ineffective instrument for general government, because under this constitution each State was in many ways a separate nation unto itself, united to the other States only insofar as that was convenient.

For example, some of the biggest States were taxing goods shipped through their ports by adjacent smaller States as if the goods originated in a foreign country. Also, under the Articles of Confederation, funds to meet the expenses of general government were erratic and inadequate because the Confederation Congress had no taxation authority. It could only request the States to contribute the needed money to run the general government, and some States were paying the amount requested while others made only partial payment or none at all, which naturally angered the States that paid the full amount requested. Moreover, the Articles of Confederation required every State's consent to amend it and the agreement of nine of the thirteen States to enact laws. There was no presiding officer to see that national laws, once passed, were executed, nor were there any national courts to adjudicate interstate disputes.

The reason for such an impotent general government was obviously the experiences the colonies had in 1757-1775 with the imperious, overbearing government of Britain. Americans did not want to submit again to a government that claimed to have power to change the constitution without their consent. Therefore, the Articles of Confederation and Perpetual Union made each State as autonomous as possible. Under the government instituted by the Articles, the newly independent United States seemed headed for the collapse which Europe's aristocratic governments predicted for it. Even in America, some of the most prominent veterans of the War for Independence and most distinguished patriots agreed that the Union was in peril and a radical reform of the constitution for general government was urgently needed.

Hence a convention of delegates from twelve of the thirteen States spent the summer of 1787 (May 25-September 17) behind sentry-guarded doors in Philadelphia's State House (now called Independence Hall) debating the provisions for an equitable general government that would justly serve the interests of all the States and their sovereign peoples. The delegates to the Constitutional Convention in Philadelphia, no matter what their views were on particular issues, were determined to achieve that goal and to protect the God-given birthright to freedom of every American. There had to be a way, they believed, for patriots of goodwill who recognized the need for unity to create a stronger Union of the States that would provide security for them all and be of equal benefit to them while preserving the freedom of themselves and future generations.

It was *not* their purpose to create a government that would decide as it went along (in some "evolutionary" way) what its powers were with each new deal of the political cards and change of circumstances— the present-day doctrine of "a Living Constitution" which bears a strong resemblance to the way George the Third and the British Parliament behaved in 1757-1775. The patriots who framed the Constitution of the United States in 1787 wanted a national government of limited, enumerated powers, spelled out in writing and approved by the people of the States. They did not want to construct a writ for general chicanery and self-aggrandizement by those "in power'—which is to say, in office. And after four months of debate, conducted in a spirit of patriotism and mutual respect, that was the kind of Union the framers did in fact create: a constitutional government that literate Americans of mature experience and common sense could understand and serve in with pride if elected or appointed to it, a government of "laws not men," as they liked to say.

The way this constitution was ratified shows how much it reflects the will of the people of the States. First, the framers of the proposed constitution sent it to the Confederation Congress in New York which, on February 21, 1787, had authorized the Constitutional Convention in Philadelphia and had instructed it to "render the federal constitution adequate to the exigencies of Government & the preservation of the Union."[3] Accompanying the proposed constitution's text was a cover letter, unanimously approved by the signers of the constitution, advising that it be: "submitted to a convention of delegates, chosen in each State by the people thereof, under the recommendation of its legislature, for their assent."[4] The Confederation Congress, on receiving the proposed constitution and the cover letter, discussed both and then forwarded the constitution, as the cover letter recommended, to the thirteen State legislatures for their consideration. All thirteen of the State legislatures discussed the proposed new constitution, and each of them authorized the election of the special State Ratification Conventions the convention in Philadelphia had recommended in its cover letter. These special conventions made the final decision, State by State, on whether to approve or to reject the proposed constitution for a new kind of Union and general government for the States. In the end, all thirteen of these single-purpose elected assemblies approved the government required by the Constitution of the United States.

At the Constitutional Convention in Philadelphia, James

---

3 "Resolution of Congress February 21, 1787," in Carl Van Doren, *The Great Rehearsal: The Story of the Making and Ratifying of the Constitution of the United States* (Viking Press, 1948), 264.
4 "Resolution of the Convention, September 17, 1787." Ibid., 310.

Madison was the chief promoter of the idea of ratification by the people of the States acting through specially elected conventions in their respective States. He spoke to this issue three times: first on June 5 in the Convention's second week; again, halfway through the Convention on July 23; and on August 31, three weeks before the end of the Convention. The first time Madison addressed this crucial matter of how the new constitution should be approved, he said it was "indispensable that the new Constitution should be ratified in the most unexceptionable form, and by the supreme authority of the people" of the States, from whose sovereign power all of the State constitutions had derived and which was the proper source of authority for the new constitution for national government. Otherwise, the constitution they were framing would lack compelling authority, for the main deficiency of the Articles of Confederation had been that it had been approved by State legislatures which meant, Madison argued, that it lacked the standing with the people of the States it would have had, had they ratified it.

On July 23, when Madison rose for the second time to address his fellow delegates on this fundamental question, he stated once more that "ratification must of necessity be obtained from the people" of the States. He argued this time that "the difference between a system founded on the Legislatures only, and one founded on the people" is "the true difference between a *league or treaty*, and a *Constitution*." Judges might, he said, regard the violation of a treaty "unwise or perfidious," but a law that violated "a constitution established by the people themselves, would be considered by the Judges as null & void." In his final remarks on the matter of ratification toward the end of the Constitutional Convention, Madison pointed out that ratification by the people of the States would be best because "The people were, in fact, the fountain of all power, and by resorting to them, all difficulties were got over. They could alter constitutions as they please." Ratification by the people of the States would be, he said, a resort to "first principles."[5] It was Madison's contention that only representatives chosen by the people of the United States for the special purpose of ratification could rightly say whether they were willing to live under a constitution as radically different from the Articles of Confederation as the one the Philadelphia Convention had constructed. Madison's arguments for ratification by the people of the States prevailed. That was the means finally agreed on by unanimous vote of the signers of the proposed constitution to give it proper authority.

The Confederation Congress, which received that recommendation, could have aborted the whole ratification process by deciding that the Constitutional Convention in Philadelphia, in writing a new constitution instead of amending the Articles of Confederation, had exceeded its authority and refusing to send the proposed constitution to the States for consideration. But that did not happen. The Confederation Congress forwarded the proposed constitution it received from the Philadelphia Convention to the State legislatures, as the Convention's cover letter recommended. Nor did any of the State legislatures, when they received the proposed new constitution from the Confederation Congress, refuse to authorize the election of a State Ratification Convention to make the final determination about it. Thus *twenty-seven* bodies of representatives of the people of the States (the thirteen State legislatures, the Confederation Congress, and the thirteen specially-elected State Ratification Conventions) reviewed the proposed constitution. And in each case, these twenty-seven representative bodies consented to the process by which the new constitution was finally considered and authorized by the people of all thirteen States of the United States.

---

5 *Notes of Debates in the Federal Convention of 1787,* 70, 352-353, 564.

Every time the people of a territory of the United States have voted to become a State and have petitioned Congress to join the Union, they have been agreeing to live under the general government established in the Constitution of the United States. Thus, the people of the fifty States have each given their sovereign authority to the requirements of the Constitution. The most recent of these ratifications was by the people of Hawaii when they joined the Union in 1959 as the fiftieth State.

However, during the ratification of the U. S. Constitution by the original thirteen States, something else besides mere approval happened. Several State Ratification Conventions were apprehensive that the new constitution would encroach on the personal liberties and rights of the people of the States because it established a much more powerful national government than the Articles of Confederation allowed. They therefore insisted that a Bill of Rights be added to the Constitution to protect the personal liberties and rights of the people of the States from federal encroachment. (North Carolina, by a 184 to 84 vote of its State Ratification Convention, initially refused to approve the proposed constitution unless a Bill of Rights was added to it.) Some States—including three of the four largest: Massachusetts, New York, and Virginia—ratified but made specific recommendations for the wanted Bill of Rights. In all, the State Ratification Conventions made more than one hundred written proposals for the addition of a Bill of Rights. Many of these proposals were, of course, redundant.[6]

The demand for the addition of a Bill of Rights was so insistent among the people of the States that two-thirds of both houses of the First Congress elected under the authority of the new constitution during their First Session wrote a set of twelve amendments and sent them out to the States on September 25,

6 Sol Bloom, *The Story of the Constitution, United States Constitution Sesquicentennial Commission* (Washington, D. C., 1937), 166.

1789, for ratification as the wanted Bill of Rights. Ten of these twelve amendments were approved by three-fourths of the State legislatures, as required by Article V, and became part of the Constitution of the United States on December 15, 1791. Because of when this Bill of Rights was created, the circumstances of its creation, and the fact that it concerns a single subject (limiting the general government's powers, particularly with regard to personal liberties and rights), the Bill of Rights ought to be thought of and construed as part of the Constitution's original framing: an eighth Article added at the insistence of the people of the States to the other seven Articles of the Constitution that were drafted in Philadelphia in 1787.

The purpose of this set of amendments (the Bill of Rights) is explained in the preamble Congress prepared and sent to the States with the proposed amendments on September 25, 1789. It reads:

> The Conventions of a number of States, having at the time of their adopting the Constitution, expressed a desire, *in order to prevent misconstruction or abuse of its powers, that further declaratory and restrictive clauses should be added:* And as extending the ground of public confidence in the Government will best ensure the beneficent ends of its institution.
>
> RESOLVED by the Senate and House of Representatives of the United States of America, in Congress assembled, two thirds of both Houses concurring, that the following Articles be proposed to the Legislatures of the several States, as amendments to the Constitution of the United States .... (italics added)[7]

The Bill's first eight amendments enumerate twenty-six personal rights and liberties: freedom of religion, freedom of speech,

---

7   *The Constitution of the United States: The Full Text with Supplementary Materials,* ed. Rob Blaisdell (Dover Publiclations, 2009), 153.

the right to keep and bear arms, the right to be immune from unwarranted searches and seizures, the right to trial by jury, etc. These personal rights and liberties are put by the Bill under the exclusive jurisdiction of the States. A Supreme Court decision in 1833 written by U. S. Chief Justice John Marshall recognized this restriction on federal authority. In *Barron v. Baltimore*, 7 Pet. (32 U. S.) 243 (1833), Marshall, who knew several of the Constitution's framers and had himself been a leading delegate to Virginia's Ratification Convention, declared that the function of the Bill of Rights was to protect the people of the States "against the apprehended encroachments of the general government." Marshall also rightly noted in *Barron v. Baltimore* that there is "no expression" in the Bill of Rights granting the general government any authority over the personal liberties and rights enumerated in it. Rather, the States have sole jurisdiction over disputes arising from these rights and liberties. Thus, the separation of power between the States and the general government set forth in Sections 8, 9, and 10 of Article I in the U. S. Constitution was continued in the Bill of Rights.

The Ninth and Tenth Amendments in the Bill of Rights have the same restrictive purpose. These amendments provide *rules* for separating the general government's authority from the authority of the States. The Ninth Amendment forbids the federal government from ever deciding what the rights of the people of the States are: "The enumeration in the Constitution of certain rights shall not be construed to deny or disparage others retained by the people." Only the sovereign people of the States can determine and declare their personal rights and liberties. Likewise, the Tenth Amendment is a further restriction on the national government: "The powers not delegated to the United States by the Constitution, nor prohibited by it to the States, are reserved to the States respectively or to the people." The Tenth Amendment defines the principle of the separation of powers which is the main organizing principle in the Constitution of the United States. The Amendment's purpose is to protect the people of the States from an unconstitutional enlargement of the general government's authority.

In reading the Constitution, it is essential to notice that all eight of its Articles (considering the Bill of Rights to be the eighth Article) are based on the principle of the separation of powers. That separation was the means the framers used and the people of the fifty States have approved to forestall arbitrary federal behavior of the sort that the king and parliament of Britain tried to exert in 1757-1775.

In the Constitution of the United States, for instance, the legislative branch has no authority to pass judgment on the constitutionality of the laws it enacts; nor can it execute those laws. Those functions are assigned respectively to the U. S. government's judicial and executive branches. In the British constitution, the principal members of the executive branch of the national government (the Prime Minister and the ministers of the numerous departments under his authority) are members of Parliament and can both introduce and vote on bills. There is no separation of executive and legislative power. In addition, the British constitution has no judicial branch. Most significantly, no branch of the government of the United States can amend the U. S. Constitution: Article V vests the power to amend exclusively in the people of the States, each State having a single vote. Indeed, in the U S. Constitution, no branch of the general government except Congress can even *propose* an amendment, let alone authorize one. In the British constitution, the House of Commons has the sole power to amend it. In the United States, the national government is organized around a division of authority between the general government and the State governments in which the people of the States remain the sovereign power of government at both the State and the national levels.

To further check the power of the general government, it is divided into three branches, each having a primary responsibility (legislative, executive, and judicial) distinct from the other two. To curb still more the general government's potential for usurping power, its legislative branch (the Congress) which was intended by the Constitution's framers to be the most powerful branch of the national government is divided into two houses: a House of Representatives, representing the people of the States in proportion to their respective populations and a Senate, representing their equal sovereignty. These legislative divisions must concur in specified ways to enact a national law (the process is spelled out in Article I, Section 7).

The primary importance of the States is likewise indicated in the name the Declaration of Independence bestowed on the country: the United States of America. In this name, *States* is the substantive. *United* and *of America* particularize the States.

The wording of the Constitution's Preamble likewise indicates the primary importance of the States. The Preamble's first draft, reported to the Constitutional Convention on August 6, 1787, read: "We the people of the States of New Hampshire, Massachusetts, Rhode-Island and Providence Plantations, Connecticut, New-York, New-Jersey, Pennsylvania, Delaware, Maryland, Virginia, North-Carolina, South-Carolina, and Georgia, do ordain, declare, and establish the following Constitution for the Government of Ourselves and our Posterity."[8] The Preamble's second draft, signed as part of the final wording of the Constitution's text on September 17, 1787, reads: "We the people of the United States ... do ordain and establish this Constitution for the United States of America" because the framers realized, in considering the initial wording of the Preamble, that no one could be certain all thirteen States named in that

---

8 *Notes of Debates in the Federal Convention of 1787*, 385.

draft would in fact ratify the Constitution. More importantly, the framers realized not-yet-settled, not-yet-named States would be joining the Union (Article IV, Section 3) and that to omit reference to the people of those as-yet-unnamed, future States and not cite their authorization of the Constitution would be a mistake. Hence, the naming of States in the Preamble was dropped and the all-inclusive reference: "We the people of the United States" (meaning the people of the States who approve the Constitution in joining the Union) was substituted for the naming of States. In both its initial and final wordings, however, the Preamble is invoking the government-making, sovereign power of the people of the States as the constituting authority.

The final wording of the Preamble declares that the Constitution has been written to form "a more perfect Union" of the States, "establish Justice" among the States, "insure domestic Tranquility" in the States, "provide for the common defense" of the States, and promote the States' "general Welfare," so the people living in the States and their posterity can enjoy "the Blessings of Liberty" in perpetual security. The general government has no powers apart from those the sovereign people of the States have authorized in ratifying the Constitution of the United States fifty times.

The people of the States have given the Constitution of the United States its authority. It belongs to them. It does not belong to the administrators the sovereign people of the States put in office to serve them by carrying out the requirements of the Constitution they have consented to live under. Those in office in the general government are powerless except for the particular powers delegated to them in the Constitution, which they are required to uphold in all its requirements.

No person in office in the general government can amend the Constitution of the United States under color of interpreting it. No member of the federal government may pick and chose which requirements of the Constitution or which laws enacted under its authority he will uphold and which he will ignore. Nor may a member of the federal government interpret one clause in the Constitution to diminish the requirement in some other clause. For any officer of the general government to behave in any of these ways would be a high crime against the Constitution and subject him to impeachment and (if proven guilty of such disobedience) to removal from office and possible prosecution (Article II, Section 4).

The national government has no jurisdiction in all cases whatsoever. It is constrained and restricted in what it can and cannot do by the provisions, procedures, prohibitions, and principles of the Constitution. The States and the sovereign people of the States, on the other hand, do have in accordance with the ninth and tenth sections of the Bill of Rights (Amendments IX and X) reserved, unenumerated powers.

The creation without bloodshed of a new constitution for national government by consent of the people to be governed by it, as happened in America in replacing the Articles of Confederation and Perpetual Union because it proved unworkable, was unprecedented. The existence of American culture made that fundamental, bloodless improvement in government possible. The ratified, amended Constitution the people of the States of the United States authorized in 1787-1791 mirrors their cultural commitment to majority rule, the equal sovereignty of the people of the States, and the need to take into account the human tendency to abuse power, while also protecting the rights God has bestowed on man as the only creature in his Creation which he made "in his own image" (Genesis 1:26). This phrase may have reference to God's and man's shared capacity for deliberate design and creativity.

Chapter Five

THE RELIGION
OF AMERICA

Under the English constitution prior to 1829, Roman Catholics and Protestants who were not members of England's state religion (the Church of England) were ineligible to hold government office and prior to 1856 could not take degrees at the universities of Oxford and Cambridge.[1] Even in the twentieth century, Church and State in England were still so united that a change the Church of England wanted to make to its Common Book of Prayer required the permission of the British Parliament, some of whose members were atheists.[2] To this day, the head of state of England (the monarch) remains the head of the Church of England. While the constitution of England has never separated Church and State, America has never had a nationally established church. (Today's attacks on religion in America are not for the purpose of separating Church and State but to deconstruct American culture.)

One of the most exceptional features of that part of the Western Hemisphere which became the United States of America has

---

1 David Thomson, *England in the Nineteenth Century 1815-1 914*, (Penguin, 1950), 58-62.
2 Raymond Leslie Buell, *Europe: A History of Ten Years* (Macmillan, 1929), 150-53.

been its extraordinary diversity of religions. From early in its colonial history, America has been a gathering place for Protestants who were being persecuted for their religious beliefs in their European homelands. Among the early immigrants to America were also a small number of Roman Catholics, and their numbers in America swelled during the course of the nineteenth and twentieth centuries from increasing Catholic immigration and the large families Catholics often have, so that today Roman Catholics are the most numerous Christian denomination in the United States. The synagogues existing in colonial Newport, Philadelphia, and Charleston are also noteworthy, and the number of Judeo immigrants likewise increased considerably in the nineteenth and twentieth centuries as Jews fled persecutions in Russia, Germany, and other countries of Europe, persecutions which sometimes included government-sponsored genocide.

America, then, has been distinct from Europe and from other places of European settlement in the Western Hemisphere in having adherents of many religious beliefs, who found they could worship God in this country in peace and security according to their chosen practices. Early in his presidency, George Washington in his letter "To the Hebrew Congregation in Newport, Rhode Island," responding to an expression of good will from that congretation, said he expected that every American would always have religious freedom and be able to "sit in safety under his own vine and fig tree."[3]

Government screening of immigrants to ensure religious uniformity in colonial Spanish America, Brazil, and Canada and laws in those colonies forbidding the practice of any religion but Roman Catholicism prevented their development of the religious pluralism that characterized America's history from the beginning. The extraordinary multitude of religions in America

---

3   August 18, 1790. *George Washington Writings*, 76.

which resulted from the English crown's policy of not requiring immigrants to its colonies to be members of England's established state church protected all denominations of religion in America from persecution. Because there has never been a nationwide, established state church in America, no religion has ever suffered national persecution. Some colony (or State) in which a person might practice his religion unmolested without being compelled by law to pay taxes in support of a church established by law was always available. America's extraordinary variety of Christian denominations made religious tolerance greater in America than in Europe, which was one of the principal reasons America was attractive to European immigrants.

The World Almanac and Book of Facts 2015 (pp. 699-700) lists 182 religions in the United States, with more than 40,000 adherents. If every religious group below 40,000 and every one of the unaffiliated churches having autonomous memberships in the hundreds, or less, were tallied, the number of religions in America would be many times greater than 182. Churches reporting adherents of 40,000 or more range from the Church of God General Conference with 40,000 members and the World Missionary Church with 40,700 members to over 45 million members for the Southern Baptist Convention and more than 70 million for the Roman Catholic Church. The membership listed in this survey for Judaism (5,243,000) is 1.7 percent of the U.S. population of 316 million given in this annual reference book for the year 2013 (p. 607). The membership for both Islam (4,419,000) and Buddhism (4,143,000) is a bit over 1 percent.

Of course, there has been no absolute absence of prejudice or violence in the religious history of America. Religion is too important to human beings to have historically allowed an absolute religious tolerance and a perfect acceptance of all faiths equally on the part of every American. (It might be well to remark here that atheists have organized what could be termed secular churches—clubs, societies, associations, etc.—devoted to the worship of atheism and doctrinaire rationalism; and these organizations can be vehemently intolerant and aggressive toward religion in the conventional sense.) The execution of a handful of Quakers and twenty "witches" in seventeenth-century Massachusetts plus the burning down of a convent of the Roman Catholic Church in Boston in the nineteenth century hardly qualify as a history of religious intolerance and violent suppression of freedom of religion when compared to the religious persecutions and wars in sixteenth-century England, France, Spain, and Germany. In those instances, tens of thousands were killed. The slaughter of Jews that occurred in Russia and Germany in the nineteenth and twentieth centuries was in the millions.

There has been only one religious persecution in American history worth mentioning: the unrelenting intolerance toward Mormons (the Church of Jesus Christ of Latter-Day Saints) largely, it appears, because polygamous marriage formed part of the initial theology of Mormonism. Members of this church were driven out of upstate New York, where Mormonism originated in 1830, to Ohio; then to Illinois and Missouri and finally, in 1846-1847, to the far distant wilderness of Utah Territory, where Mormons finally found in that unsettled western territory of the United States the refuge they needed to practice their faith unmolested. Except for this decades-long harassment of the Church of Jesus Christ of Latter-Day Saints, which was often violent, differences of religion in America have not produced anything like the scale of religious persecution one finds over the centuries in the pages of European history, most recently in the murderous hatred of Protestants and Catholics in Northern Ireland from 1969 to 1997.

In the entire four centuries of America's history, there has never been a religious war. The complete absence of such warfare in America is one of the most exceptional features of

America's cultural history. The recurring wars and armed conflicts between American Indians and European immigrants and their descendants that continued across the entire continent down to the early twentieth century in California was over land, not religion, though religious differences on occasion, as in the Pequot War in Massachusetts and Connecticut (1636-1637), were alleged to have had something to do with these conflicts. The history of the Cherokee suggests their true cause, for when the Cherokee under the leadership of their great chief Sequoyah (c. 1770-1843) embraced Christianity, created a written language, started a newspaper, published parts of the Bible in Cherokee, and adopted other American ways, Cherokee lands were still taken. Similarly, burning churches of black Americans had nothing essential to do with religion and everything to do with racial enmity. Torching sacred Negro property expressed the deep hatred some white Americans felt toward black Americans.

The kings of Spain, Portugal, and France saw to it that Roman Catholicism was, as a matter of law, the only religion practiced in their American domains. In the history of Western civilization, the passage of a government law has always been necessary to establish a religion until a U.S. Supreme Court justice capriciously held that a religious establishment could exist without a government-enacted establishment law.

Before 1947 in America, religious establishment meant a government-enacted law which made one religion, named in the law, the official mode of worship of that government and conferred on it some benefit or benefits which only a government can bestow, such as funding from public revenues or making membership in the established religion a qualification to vote and hold public office. Whatever the government benefit might be, the establishment law withheld it from atheists and anyone else who did not worship God according to the prescribed practices of the established religion.

In neither America's colonial nor its national period was there an establishment of religion encompassing every colony or State. Indeed, Article VI, paragraph three, of the U.S. Constitution prohibits making religion a qualification for national office: "[N]o religious Test shall ever be required as a Qualification to any Office or public Trust under the United States." But that prohibition did not satisfy the people of the States. It seemed an insufficient guarantee of their religious freedom, and they insisted on putting into the Bill of Rights requirements prohibiting the federal government from having any jurisdiction over religious matters. This restriction on federal jurisdiction is stated in the First Amendment of the Bill of Rights: "Congress shall make no law respecting an establishment of religion, or prohibiting the free exercise thereof." The choice of the word "respecting" forbad the government of the United States from establishing a religion by law *and* from disturbing any of the seven religious establishment laws then extant and in effect in the States of the United States.

The State establishment laws in effect when the First Amendment was written and ratified (1789-1791) established the Protestant religion in New Hampshire, New Jersey, and South Carolina; Christianity in Maryland and Delaware; and the Congregational Church in Massachusetts and Connecticut. All seven of these State laws mandated that ministers of the religions which they established be supported from public revenues. Ministers of other religions were excluded from receiving this benefit. The strongest of the seven State religious establishments, those of Massachusetts and Connecticut, also made membership in the Congregational Church a requirement for voting and holding public office. By 1833, Connecticut, Delaware, Maryland, Massachusetts, New Hampshire, New Jersey, and South Carolina had all rescinded their establishment laws; and no State since that date has enacted an establishment law. Hence, for almost two centuries now, there have been no religious establishments in the United States.

The board of education for the State of New York in approving a nondenominational prayer for voluntary recitation in the State's public schools as part of "the moral education" of students was not establishing a religion in the State of New York as the U.S. Supreme Court in 1962 claimed it was. George Washington took notice of the connection between religion and morality in his "Farewell Address" in these terms:

> Of all the dispositions and habits which lead to political prosperity [i.e. success], Religion and morality are indispensable supports. In vain would that man claim the tribute of Patriotism, who should labour to subvert these great Pillars of human happiness, these firmest props of the duties of Men and citizens.... Whatever may be conceded to the influence of refined education on minds of peculiar structure, reason and experience both forbid us to expect that National morality can prevail in exclusion of religious principle.[4]

The twenty-two-word prayer the New York State board of education recommended for voluntary use in the State's public schools: "Almighty God, we acknowledge our dependence upon Thee, and we beg Thy blessings upon us, our parents, our teachers, and our Country," simply acknowledged the dependence of Americans on God as the source of blessings. The New York board of education in recommending this simple prayer for voluntary recitation was not naming a particular religion as the State government's mode of worship. Nor did it confer on students who recited the prayer any government benefit which was withheld from students who did not recite the prayer.

Nevertheless, the U. S. Supreme Court in *Engel v. Vitale*, 370

---

4 *George Washington Writings*, 971.

U. S. 421 (1962), declared that the New York State school board, in approving a non-denominational prayer which taught that God exists and is the source of blessings and recommending its voluntary recitation in New York public schools for the moral education of students, had established a religion in violation of the First Amendment's establishment clause. This 1962 decision by the Supreme Court was, of course, a nationwide ban on prayer in public schools, because whatever is deemed unconstitutional in one State is unconstitutional in every State. The following year (1963), the Supreme Court accepted on appeal a case regarding Bible-reading in public schools and also banned that exercise of religion and not long afterwards likewise banned the display of the Ten Commandments on public school property.

But no federal judge can alter the history of religious establishments. Nor can any federal court amend the U.S. Constitution by interpreting it. Nor can any federal court legitimately exercise a power not granted to it in the Constitution.

In justification of its 1962 school prayer decision, the Supreme Court quoted from the write up of a 1947 case that also dealt with religion and public schools which had come to the Court on appeal: *Everson v. Board of Education of Ewing Township*, 330 U.S. 1 (1947). In that case the plaintiff, Arch Everson, claimed a New Jersey law allowing the transportation of students to parochial schools (i.e. church schools) at the State's expense was an establishment of religion. But the Supreme Court held that the New Jersey law had *not* established a religion in providing for the transportation of students to religious schools at public expense because no one religion was being singled out for preferential treatment. All parochial schools in the State were being treated the same. No religion's schools were being excluded from receiving the benefit from the State of New Jersey. The Court's reasoning in *Everson v. Board of Education of Ewing Township* was in perfect accord with the historic definition of religious establishments.

But in writing up that 1947 Supreme Court decision, Associate Justice Hugo Lafayette Black inserted his idiosyncratic definitions of religious establishment which disregarded history. Black made four assertions:

> The "establishment of religion" clause in the First Amendment means at least this: Neither a state nor the Federal Government can set up a church. Neither can pass laws which aid one religion, aid all religions, or prefer one religion over another.

The first of these assertions was historically invalid because it was true only of the federal government. It did not apply to the federal government *and* the States because half the States in the United States had religious establishment laws when the First Amendment was written and ratified in 1789-1791; and these seven establishment laws remained in effect until the States that had enacted them rescinded them. The last establishment law was rescinded by the Massachusetts legislature in 1833. Thus, for the first forty-two years the First Amendment was in effect as part of the Constitution of the United States, one or more States had an establishment of religion because the First Amendment does not forbid a State from establishing a religion. It forbids only *Congress* from establishing a religion.

Justice Black's second and fourth propositions—that neither the governments of the States nor the national government "can pass laws which aid one religion" or "prefer one religion over another"—are likewise invalid because the First Amendment prohibits only Congress from making a law aiding one religion in preference to all other religions, a law which half the States in the Union had when the First Amendment was ratified. Black's third proposition—that neither a State nor the federal government can "aid all religions"—was, by far, the most astounding of his four assertions, since it contradicted the Court's finding in *Everson* which Black was writing up. The Court in this case had decided that New Jersey had *not* established a religion in transporting students to religious schools at State expense precisely because it was providing the service to *all religions* without preference for any *one* religion.

Black's claim that government aid to all religions is an establishment of religion not only contradicted the Supreme Court's own finding in *Everson v. Board of Education* which he was writing up but the very purpose of religious establishments wherever they have been found throughout history, including U. S. history. The whole point of making a religious establishment is to aid one religion. Such laws never "aid all religions."

In publishing in 1947 the four nonsensical assertions Black made in writing up the verdict in *Everson v. Board of Education*, the Supreme Court made his nonsense into judicial precedents which could be cited in future cases and were so cited by the Court fifteen years later, in its 1962 ban on school prayer (*Engel v. Vitale*). By citing, in 1962, Black's erroneous assertions of 1947, the Supreme Court condoned his errors, so that since 1962 all signs of respect for belief in God, the foundational belief of America's culture, have been banned from public school education in the United States.

But citing Black's nonsensical assertions about religious establishments has not been the Supreme Court's only error regarding religion. By taking *Everson v. Board of Education* in 1947 and *Engel v. Vitale* in 1962 for appellate review, the Court exercised jurisdiction in religious matters and thus violated the First Amendment's exclusion of the federal government from having jurisdiction in religious matters and violated Article V which forbids any branch of the federal government to amend the Constitution.

Egregious as those acts were, the U. S. Supreme Court committed yet another, worse violation of constitutional jurisprudence in claiming in *Engel v. Vitale* (1962) that a free recitation of a nondenominational prayer was a religious establishment. By citing in that decision the First Amendment's establishment clause and Hugo Black's preposterous 1947 assertion that aid to "all religions" is an establishment of religion, the Supreme Court canceled the First Amendment's clause protecting "the free exercise" of religion. In short, the Supreme Court used one clause in the Constitution (the establishment clause) to abrogate another clause (the free exercise clause) and thus violated the integrity of the Constitution. The Court ignored the fact that the First Amendment's religious clauses ("Congress shall make no law respecting an establishment of religion, or prohibiting the free exercise thereof") are coordinate requirements, designed in tandem to exclude the federal government from having any jurisdiction in matters of religion and giving that jurisdiction solely to the States. The First Amendment's religious clauses are coordinate limitations on the federal government in regard to religious freedom.

Thomas Jefferson forthrightly expressed that understanding of the First Amendment when he said in 1805 in his Second Inaugural Address as U. S. President: "In matters of religion, I have considered its free exercise is placed by the Constitution independent of the powers of the general government."[5] This is Jefferson's most public declaration on the relation between government and religion in the United States: the essence of his thinking on the subject of the separation of Church and State.

In writing up the Supreme Court's decision in *Everson* (1947), Hugo Black never mentioned Jefferson's declaration that the religious clauses in the First Amendment exclude the federal government from having any jurisdiction in matters of religion. The Supreme Court in exercising such jurisdiction again in *Engel* (1962) agreed with the plaintiffs that a religious

---

5   *Thomas Jefferson Writings*, 519-520.

exercise which offended their religious sensibilities could not be protected by the U.S. Constitution. Thus the feelings of the plaintiffs in that case were given greater consideration by the Supreme Court than the feelings of the majority of parents in the State of New York, who wanted their children to be taught that God exists through reciting a simple prayer to that effect. To ban from America's public schools, as the Court did, all signs of respect for belief in God on the grounds that it was offensive to some persons, was to ban every expression of religious belief, because there are no religious sentiments which will not be offensive to someone.

The will of the people of the States, as expressed in the First Amendment, is that the federal government shall have no jurisdiction over religion. The Supreme Court has claimed to have such jurisdiction through a false interpretation of the Fourteenth Amendment known as "the Incorporation Doctrine." This Doctrine was instituted by the efforts of Supreme Court Justice Hugo Black who tenaciously asserted in the 1940s, 50s, and 60s that the Fourteenth Amendment in 1868 had transferred jurisdiction over religion and the rest of the personal liberties of the Bill of Rights from the States to the U.S. government. This is what Section 1 of the Amendment says:

> *All persons* born or naturalized in the United States, and subject to the jurisdiction thereof, are citizens of the United States and of the State wherein they reside. No State shall make or enforce any law which shall abridge the privileges or immunities of citizens of the United States; nor shall any State deprive *any person* of life, liberty, or property, without due process of law; nor deny to *any person* within its jurisdiction the *equal protection* of the law (italics added).

Section 5 of the Fourteenth Amendment declares: "The Congress shall have power to enforce, by appropriate legislation, the provisions of this article [of amendment]." This same concluding clause empowering Congress to enforce the Fourteenth Amendment's requirements is also found in the Thirteenth Amendment (1865) abolishing slavery and the Fifteenth Amendment (1870) conferring the right to vote on U.S. citizens regardless of "race, color, or previous condition of servitude."All three of these Amendments (XIII, XIV, XV) were written and ratified in consequence of the Civil War and the intent of Section 1 of the Fourteenth Amendment was to give black Americans the same rights, the same privileges, the same liberties, the same immunities, and the same protection of the law as white Americans. Section 5 of the Fourteenth Amendment put these new rights, privileges, liberties, and immunities for this specific part of the American population (black Americans) under federal protection.[6]

This race-specific intention of the First Section of the Fourteenth Amendment becomes convincingly clear by asking one simple question: Were white Americans born or naturalized in Pennsylvania, say, and subject to the jurisdiction of the United States being declared citizens of the United States and of Pennsylvania through ratification of the Fourteenth Amendment in 1868? Clearly not. They already had such citizenship. Nor were the white citizens of Pennsylvania (or any other State) being granted equal protection of the law by ratification of the Fourteenth Amendment, which they already had. The diction "All persons," "any person," and "equal protection" in Section 1 of the Fourteenth Amendment and the grant of power to Congress in Section 5 to enforce the Amendment were manifestly

---

6 This same provision, "The Congress shall have power to enforce this article by appropriate legislation," occurs in Amendments XIX (1920), XXIII (1961), and XXIV (1964) concerning qualifications to vote for specifically defined demographic groups (women and persons eighteen years old) and prohibiting poll taxes in order to vote; all of which amended the authority of the States, granted in Article I, Section 2 of the Constitution, to determine qualifications for voting.

references to black Americans in conferring full citizenship on them. Federal protection was needed to prevent any State from denying them their enjoyment of their new rights as full citizens of the United States and of the States wherein they resided, rights the Bill of Rights had previously extended to white citizens. The Fourteenth Amendment was conferring citizenship on a particular group of Americans.

The former slaves emancipated by the Thirteenth Amendment, and the naturalized and freeborn black Americans who had been denied by State laws in the States where they resided the equal citizenship that white Americans born or naturalized in the United States enjoyed, were granted that equality by the Civil War Amendments (XIII, XIV, XV) ratified in 1865-1870. The Fourteenth Amendment gave these naturalized, freeborn, and emancipated black Americans the special protection of the U. S. government, because the eleven States which had seceded from the Union to perpetuate the institution of chattel slavery and had been defeated in the war could not be trusted to protect their rights. Nor could other States which before the war had withheld the rights of citizenship from *freeborn* and *naturalized* black Americans be trusted to protect their rights. Therefore, a special power had to be granted to Congress for the protection of freeborn, naturalized, and emancipated black Americans. Section 1 of the Fourteenth Amendment did not make native born and naturalized white Americans who were subject to the jurisdiction of the United States citizens of the United States and of "the State in which they reside." It did that for black Americans.

Nonetheless, Hugo Lafayette Black chose to ignore this meaning of the Fourteenth Amendment and insisted in his "Incorporation Doctrine" that Sections 1 and 5 of the Fourteenth Amendment had transferred complete and absolute protection of the personal rights and liberties of *every* American to the U.S. government. The historical context in which the terms "All," "any," and "equal protection" are used in Section 1 of the Fourteenth Amendment (the post-Civil War context of 1865-1870 in which this Amendment and the Thirteenth and Fifteenth Amendments were ratified) meant nothing to Hugo Black or to the supporters of his Incorporation Doctrine. As New Dealers, they were interested only in removing constitutional limitations on federal jurisdiction. They wanted the federal government to have authority in all cases whatsoever and claimed through the "Incorporation Doctrine" that the Fourteenth Amendment was not intended to apply to just federal protection of black Americans. (The States that seceded from the Union were required to ratify the Fourteenth Amendment as a condition of their readmission to the Union.[7])

The "Incorporation Doctrine" is an unwarranted, bone-jarring expansion of federal authority which has had a lot to do with making the government of the United States the all-intrusive presence in the lives of Americans that it has become.

Altogether, there are nine sections in the Thirteenth, Fourteenth, and Fifteenth Amendments, all of them relating to the Civil War, the most consequential of which was granting freeborn, naturalized and formerly enslaved black Americans equal citizenship with freeborn, naturalized white Americans. But for a full century after the ratification of these amendments, Congress did not use its constitutional power to enforce the citizenship rights of black Americans as it should have done and was constitutionally obliged to do. The exercise of federal power to protect black Americans had to wait for the Christian-based, non-violent Civil Rights Movement initiated, organized, and conducted by black Americans in the 1950s and 60s to bring moral pressure to bear on the federal government to perform the constitutional responsibilities conferred on it in regard to black Americans by

---

7 John Hope Franklin, *Reconstruction After the Civil War* (University of Chicago Press, 1961), 130.

the three Civil War Amendments. The Fourteenth Amendment did not expand federal power and jurisdiction in any other way.

Americans have always made religious freedom a separate concern from freedom of speech. The free exercise of religion is not a subcategory of free speech. Rather, it is a distinct right having a fundamental importance to American culture. The argument in the Declaration of Independence makes plain the foundational necessity of belief in personal rights which come from "the Laws of Nature and Nature's God." That same belief is also expressed in George Washington's "Farewell Address" and the Northwest Ordinance. The primacy which belief in God has in American culture is likewise reflected in the fact that Americans to this day are much more inclined than the British or the French and other Europeans to engage in daily prayer, to believe God created the Universe, and to say God is "very important" to them.[8]

Tocqueville in his observations on the American way of life said this regarding religion: "On my arrival in the United States the religious aspect of the country was the first thing that struck my attention, and the longer I stayed there, the more I perceived the great political consequences resulting from this new state of things." He went on to make the further observation: "In France, I had almost always seen the spirit of religion and the spirit of freedom marching in opposite directions. But in America, I found they were intimately united and that they reigned in common over the same country."[9] Because American government has been established on the belief that God has given human beings the same rights to life, liberty, the pursuit of happiness, and government by consent of the governed

8 Results of an international poll on religion conducted by UNESCO summarized in *The Wilson Quarterly* (Winter 1996), 128.
9 *Democracy in America*, I, 319.

(Declaration of Independence, second paragraph), God's existence has for Americans an indispensable political importance.

The connection between political rights and what George Washington called "religious principle" is likewise evident in the Northwest Ordinance by which five new States (Ohio, Indiana, Illinois, Michigan, and Wisconsin) were admitted to the Union. This federal law summarized: "the fundamental principles of civil and religious liberty, which form the basis whereon these republics [i.e. the States of the United States], their laws, and constitutions are erected." Six "fundamental principles" are declared in this law enacted by the First Congress; two of them concern religion.[10]

Article 1: "No person, demeaning himself [i.e. conducting himself] in a peaceable and orderly manner, shall ever be molested on account of his mode of worship or religious sentiments, in the said territory." Article 3: "Religion, morality, and knowledge being necessary to good government and the happiness of mankind, schools and the means of education shall forever be encouraged." These principles connected religion to education, government, and happiness in America. The first declared that no mode of worship was to be considered superior to any other mode in the new States to be formed from the Northwest Territory and that no member of any church or any atheist was to be harassed because of "their [religious] sentiments." This was the principle of religious tolerance which was fundamental to America's religiously diverse culture.

Under the Ordinance's Third Article, teaching religion and morality in the public schools of the Northwest Territory was part of the education of young Americans in good government.

---

10 "The Northwest Ordinance" in *Words That Make America Great*, compiled and edited by Jerome Agel, Section Introductions by Milton J. Cantor (Random House, 1999), 75-76. The other four principles had to do with constitutionality, the rights of settlers, slavery (which the Ordinance banned in the Northwest Territory), and the stages of development for the admission of States to the Union.

This connection was sundered by the "New Deal" Supreme Court which claimed the federal government had jurisdiction over matters of religion and banned prayer, Bible reading, and the Ten Commandments from public schools.

Between 1937 and 1943, Franklin Roosevelt, appointed eight Associate Justices, starting with Hugo Black, and a new Chief Justice to the U. S. Supreme Court—an entirely new Court, all of whom were staunch New Dealers. (The new Chief Justice, Harlan Fisk Stone, was a registered Republican already on the Court as an Associate Justice who was made Chief Justice because he "most frequently voted to uphold New Deal legislation against constitutional challenge."[11]) American culture has yet to recover from the New Deal Supreme Court's usurpation of jurisdiction over religion, in which Hugo Lafayette Black played the leading role. (1) He falsified Jefferson's views on religion and government in *Everson v. Board of Education* by ignoring Jefferson's 1805 Inaugural. (2) He defined an establishment of religion in nonsensical ways in *Engel v. Vitale,* which produced false judicial precedents regarding religious establishment. And (3) he formulated the false "Incorporation Doctrine" regarding the Fourteenth Amendment, which is a de facto amendment of the Constitution putting the personal rights and liberties of every American under federal control, including matters of religious freedom. Black's falsehoods and abuses of his office spectacularly undermined the foundational role of religion in American culture.

Crossing the Atlantic to America during the first three centuries of America's history tested the faith of those brave enough to contemplate the hazards of the voyage. Faith in God could in

---

11 Albert P. Blaustein and Roy M. Mersky, *The First One Hundred Justices: Statistical Studies on the Supreme Court of the United States* (Archon Books, 1978), Table One, 106-108. *The Oxford Companion to the Supreme Court of the United States,* edited by Kermit L. Hall (Oxford University Press, 1992), 838. See also Stone's entry in *The Supreme Court Justices* (Congressional Quarterly, 1993), 364.

fact be crucial to taking that necessary first step to becoming an American, as seen in the memoir of one of these immigrants. Rebecca Burlend recounts in her memoir what happened on the day in 1831 she, her husband, and their young children were scheduled to embark at Liverpool for America. That morning, Mr. Burlend came to her from the men's dormitory where he had spent the night and announced that he didn't want to go to America. "Such another night as the last has been I cannot survive!" he said. He told her he had a "terrible anxiety" about what might befall her and the children "on the stormy ocean, or in a strange land and among pathless woods" if anything should happen to him. "Bad as our prospects are in England, we must go back!" he told her. Mrs. Burlend listened to this distraught exclamation by her husband, that he wanted to go home, even though emigration to America had been his idea, and then she calmly reminded him that they had no home to return to because they had sold everything they possessed, except what they had in their baggage, to pay for the Atlantic crossing and had given up their lease on the land they had been farming as renters. She proposed to Mr. Burlend that instead of balking, they "look to Providence" for protection and proceed with their intention to go to America. The advice (or rather the reminder) that they should trust in God, she reports, "operated like a charm" in restoring her normally optimistic husband to his usual spirits. And when the ship on which they had booked passage to America sailed, the Burlend family was aboard, "having previously confided ourselves to the care of Him whom earth and seas are ready to obey."[12]

How many times trust in God was needed to board the

---

12 *A True Picture of Emigration: or Fourteen Years in the Interior of North America: Being a Full and Impartial Account of the Various Difficulties and Ultimate Success of an English Family Who Emigrated from Barwick-in-Elmet, Near Leeds, in the Year 1831* (Citadel Press, 1974), 11-14.

wooden sailing ships that carried the first twelve generations of self-selected immigrants to America, we can only guess. But certainly the moment of embarkation to face the actual dangers of the ocean crossing and leave behind everything and everyone they had ever known or held dear must have commonly involved some degree of remorse or panic of the sort Rebecca Burlend reports afflicted her husband. At the actual point of going aboard the immigrant ships to an unknown continent, even committed immigrants may have wished to return to the safety of "home" forthwith, rather than go forward to America. The ordeal of crossing the Atlantic tended to screen out those whose trust in God was weak.

The same potentially disabling anxiety must also have afflicted the pioneers when the moment came to leave already settled, known parts of America to go in search of imagined opportunities in the unknown wilderness farther west. In all likelihood they, too, frequently had to pray to God for strength to proceed and for his protection as they left "home" for the uncertainties of the vast wilderness. We cannot know how often such prayers were needed, but undoubtedly trust in "Nature's God," the Creator of everything seen and unseen, was needed to bolster the courage of American pioneers.

The History of Plymouth Plantation by William Bradford (1590-1657), the longtime governor of the first permanent English-speaking settlement in New England, records the anxieties the Pilgrims felt on leaving Europe and their much keener anxiety in landing on the shores of eastern Massachusetts in 1620, beholding the "hideous and desolate" wilderness and realizing that they were cut off from "all civilized parts of the world." Going to America and pioneering the Stone Age wilderness of the Atlantic Coastal Plain required putting on the armor of faith in God (Ephesians 6:10-18), and the self-selected immigrants to America evidently, on the whole, had such armor to put on.

Writing in 1784, the year after America won its independence from Britain when large numbers of Americans were moving into the wilderness on the western side of the Appalachians, the 78-year-old Benjamin Franklin reported that a person could "live to a great Age" in the United States without encountering "either an Atheist or an Infidel."[13]

The significantly larger proportion of Americans, compared to Europeans, who say faith in God is important to them suggests that trust in God was indeed part of the formation of America's culture. In the UNESCO poll referred to earlier (page 100), the proportion of Americans who responded God was "very important" to them was 58 percent compared to 19 percent of respondents in Britain and 13 percent in France.

It was during the most severe trial Americans have yet faced and overcome, the Civil War, that the inscription "In God We Trust" was first put on U. S. money.

---

13 "Information to Those Who Would Remove to America," *Franklin Writings* (Library of America, 1987), 983.

Chapter Six

THE PARAMOUNT
DANGER TO AMERICA

Abraham Lincoln (1809-1865) was a young lawyer and member of the Illinois legislature when he gave a talk in 1838 to the Springfield Young Men's Lyceum on "The Perpetuation of Our Political Institutions." He began the talk by declaring that the United States occupies "the fairest portion of the earth, as regards extent of territory, fertility of soil, and salubrity of climate" and has institutions more conducive to "civil and religious liberty" than any nation ever had. He proposed to examine how these "fundamental blessings" could be lost. "If destruction be our lot," he said, "we must be its author and finisher. As a nation of freemen, we must live through all time, or die by suicide."[14] In Lincoln's judgment, Americans would enjoy their blessings forever ("through all time") as long as they remained alert to internal danger and faithful to their commitment to freedom and constitutional government. Lincoln's prescient wisdom has special meaning today, given America's history in the past half century (1965-2015).

In the 1960s, the Cold War between the United States and

---

14 *Lincoln Selected Speeches and Writings*, 13-14.

the Union of Soviet Socialist Republics following the Second World War entered a period of great danger for America with the opening of a domestic front in the struggle, manned by Americans who agreed with the Soviet goal of establishing communist regimes worldwide. (See Appendices C and D of this book which identify the conflicting values of American culture and Cultural Marxism.) The Americans who organized the domestic front in the Cold War referred to it as "the Counter-Culture Movement," or just "the Movement." It brought the conflict between the Soviet Union and the United States home to the streets and the college campuses of America. The Americans who remained true to their belief in American culture began, after a few years, referring to the Counter-Culture Movement as "Political Correctness" because of its dogmatism.

But though it is now known as Political Correctness, the movement is still committed to the goal of opposing American culture, just as it was when it was known in the 1960s as the Counter-Culture Movement. Since its inception, this movement's purpose has been to destroy America's power in the world by destroying America's culture. Launched in the 1960s, what is now called Political Correctness has persisted in attacking America's culture by promoting behaviors inimical to its beliefs. The dissolution of the Union of Soviet Socialist Republics and the Communist Party of the Soviet Union in 1989-1991 had no effect on the movement's activities. If anything, America's part in the downfall of the Soviet Union has increased the zeal of the movement's core adherents by adding a desire for revenge to their opposition of America's culture. For Marxists, America's culture remains the main obstacle to worldwide communism. Diminishing American power by "deconstructing" American culture is therefore as vital to American Marxists today as it was in the 1960s, when the domestic front in the Cold War front was opened inside the United States.

In the past half century, those Americans who want to destroy the influence of the United States in the world have worked tirelessly to destabilize American culture. They have encouraged the use of addictive drugs, pornography, and prostitution. They have derided belief in God and respect for human life. They have weakened family life. They have stimulated the growth of Big Government and dependence on it. They have redefined patriotism. Political Correctness is the kind of internal threat Abraham Lincoln warned his generation to be aware of. (In Lincoln's day, the domestic danger was the threat of secession.)

The danger which Political Correctness poses today is greater than it was in the 1960s because during the last two and a half generations, the movement has taken over one of the major political parties and infiltrated the other and is exerting an increasing influence in the nation's schools, churches, business enterprises, universities, media, governments, and philanthropic institutions. More and more, the influence of Political Correctness can be seen in court decisions, taxpayer-funded State and federal programs for "social justice," and in the everyday language used in America.

The Marxists and Marxist sympathizers who propel the PC movement today refuse to think of the United States and its history as exceptional and will not tolerate anyone who thinks that way. Quite the opposite. Marxists and Marxist sympathizers damn America and its history. They portray the United States as the world's chief oppressor and imperialist power: the principal cause of the world's social and economic problems. To give their interest in destroying America's culture an innocent air and hence lessening resistance to it, they deceitfully ask that it be accepted as simply inevitable "change." Only in rare moments of audacious candor do they remove their deceptive mask of pretending to be interested in reform and admit that what they are really after is "a new normal" and a "fundamental transformation" of America. Apart from those rare admissions, the most dangerous anti-American Americans go about their work of deception and lies with a clean-cut appearance of having only the country's well-being at heart. They speak and act in public in a way to make their fellow Americans think they are just "folks" from the same heartland of America Lincoln hailed from.

The twentieth-century Marxist revolutions in Russia, China, North Korea, Cuba, and Vietnam show the sort of thing that is in store for America if its domestic enemies triumph in their project of internal conquest through deceit. The planned socialist utopia Marxism promises has never been accomplished. It can't be. The ruthlessness required to force millions of persons to conduct themselves according to the dogmas of Cultural Marxism and the callousness needed to eliminate all political enemies strip Marxist revolutionaries of whatever normal human empathy they may have started life with.

Creating the all-powerful, uniform, one-party government that must be created to demolish existing cultures and replace them with institutions based on materialistic determinism is contrary to commonplace compassion, lawfulness, and justice. The dogmas of Marxism dehumanize those who embrace them, because Marxism in practice is government by thieves and liars. The redistribution of wealth that Marxists advocate in theory becomes in practice a criminal enterprise. Wielding total power in a totalitarian state totally corrupts those who wield it.

The Minutemen mustered at Concord and Lexington in Massachusetts that April morning of 1775 when the opening shots of the War for Independence were fired were not revolutionaries who wanted to create a new culture. Those townsmen and farmers were ordinary middle-class American workers defending the cultural beliefs by which they and previous generations of Americans had conducted their lives.

They were sons of American liberty who wanted to preserve the blessings they enjoyed as Americans. Self-government was their goal. They felt no allegiance to anything they did not freely consent to and that was not, in their judgment, consistent with the Almighty Creator's ordained laws of right and wrong. The patriots at Concord and Lexington that day were willing to freely give their lives to defend the belief-behaviors of the American way of life. They had no ambition to force anyone to participate in it. Imposing a new culture on others by force and propaganda is a defining characteristic of Marxist revolutions and regimes.

Americans, as Thomas Jefferson said in the Declaration of Independence, believe God has given all human beings the same birthright. Human beings have been created so that they act in their own best interests only when they freely choose to live in accordance with the commandments of the Being who created the universe. That is the lesson in the story of the first man and the first woman and their expulsion from the paradise God created for them, which they lost by disobeying him (Genesis, chaps. 2-3). Marxists display the same misuse of freedom as Adam and Eve. They think they can be omnipotent and all-knowing and can disregard God and his laws with impunity. They do not believe God has created physical laws to govern nature and moral laws to govern human nature.

To neutralize Marxism, people have to be convinced of the truth that God's moral laws (the Ten Commandments) are inherently necessary in the nature of things as God has created them and must be obeyed as the will of God for human well-being and human prosperity. Those desirable goals are not achieved by substituting an almighty government for Almighty God. We are free to either obey God's laws or to disobey them. Obeying God's laws frees us from *sin*, a word like the word *evil* that good Marxists never use. Marxists have made a religion of materialistic determinism and preach that salvation lies in a correct organization of the political, social, and material environment. To Marxists, Progressives, and Leftists, the hope of human salvation lies in the power of government to control the social, political, and material environment. Americans, on the other hand, believe in a higher power than government and in the freedom to choose to do what's right in the nature of things as the Almighty Creator has made them.

The communist regime of the USSR made the state all-powerful, and for a time the Soviet state seemed to triumph because of its totalitarianism. But where is Lenin's Union of Soviet Socialist Republics today? It does not exist. Nor did political and social scientists in the West who claimed to be experts on communism and Soviet government perceive that the USSR and the Communist Party of the Soviet Union would implode in 1989-1991. "The Future of the Soviet System" in *How the Soviet Union Is Governed* by Jerry F. Hough and Merle Fainsod typifies the failure of Western political and social "scientists" to foresee and predict the disintegration of the world's first country to have a full-blown Marxist government based on the philosophy of materialistic determinism.[15]

Marxism has an extraordinary track record for devastation in the name of improving human life and has been responsible for tens of millions of deaths around the world. *The Black Book of Communism: Crimes, Terror, Repression*[16] tallies the tens of millions of deaths that Marxism has been responsible for in the twentieth century in the countries where it has come to power. The death toll far exceeds that of the National Socialist German Workers' Party (the Nazis), because Hitler's attempt to establish

---

15 Harvard University Press, 1979; see pages 560-567.
16 Stephane Courtois, Nicholas Werth, Jean-Louis Panne, Andrzej Paczkowski, Karel Bartošek, Jean-Louis Margolin, Harvard University Press, 1999; translated by Jonathan Murphy and Mark Kramer. The research for this book, published first in French in 1997, uses archival materials that became available after the fall of the Soviet state.

his "Thousand Year Reich" was limited to thirteen years and one continent.

Marxists have never produced in any of the nations they have governed the wonderful "omelet" they promise to make from breaking tens of millions of eggs: the human lives they have destroyed. Marxists have too much philosophical disdain for freedom and private property to ever create and sustain a highly productive economy. All they are capable of doing through organized fear (for a time) is to intimidate masses of human beings into a show of obedience to the dogmas of Cultural Marxism. Marxist governments are based on making people act in accordance with the dictates of Marxist theory. In other words, the power of one-party communist government, wherever it exists or has existed, depends on telling the lie that it is succeeding and on making the people that it governs live in fear of what the regime can and will do to them if they do not consent to that lie. But an authentic new culture cannot be forced into being. The only people who truly benefit from a Marxist regime are its administrators, who get to satisfy their lust for self-righteousness and total power.

Marxists value theory over human life. The theory is sacred, not human beings. They say they love humanity and that the unlimited government authority which their theory of revolution requires to achieve "social justice" is only temporary and will, at some future time, "wither away." But that marvelous event, the withering away of the state, is always deferred. In the meantime, people who live under Marxist rule must put up with one-party dictatorship, lack of freedom, and chronic shortages of the amenities and necessities of civilized modern societies. There is no recorded instance of a Marxist regime ever withering away. Marxist dictatorships just get bigger and bigger and more and more corrupt and absolutist until they collapse from their own monstrous untruth.

The oppressive results of Marxist regimes and the quite opposite results of free government are clearly seen by comparing life in East and West Germany in 1949-1990 and life in present-day North and South Korea. The ethnicity of the two Germanys and the two Koreas was basically identical; their respective geographies were contiguous. Only the governments of these partitioned nations were different. West Germany and South Korea had governments based on freedom and law; East Germany and North Korea were police states justified by the supposed good that applied Marxism was doing. That one difference in political structure produced stark contrasts in life in East and West Germany and North and South Korea, contrasts which prove beyond any reasonable doubt that applied Marxism worsens rather than benefits human life.

Any practicing Christian or Jew will readily admit that material reality is part of the truth of Creation. And if material reality were (as Marxist dogma claims) the entire truth of existence, then every Marxist revolution would have produced the wonderful paradises they promised instead of the large-scale terror and death they did in fact produce. "Man does not live by bread only," the Bible says, "but by every word that proceeds from the mouth of God" (Deuteronomy 8:3). Life's essence is not matter, for matter cannot reproduce itself. God has willed the existence of life and its reproduction through laws he has created that have no material existence. These laws (God's will) did not "evolve," yet they are indispensable to life's existence and continuance. They represent the will of a Being whose nature we cannot completely comprehend. We can only observe the infinite glory of the wonders he has surrounded us with for our good and the marvelous operations of his laws, to the extent that our comprehension and resources permit. The entire unity of God's creation is beyond our understanding because God is infinite while we are not. All we can know, through faithful experience and his revelations, is that our Creator is the "I AM" of the Old Testament (Exodus 3:14) and the pre-existing "Word of God" of the New Testament (John 1:1-4).

Moses and Jesus prayed to the Creator the American Declaration of Independence invokes. Without obedience to God's divine imperatives, Marxists want to build the paradise on earth they ridicule Jews and Christians for believing once existed before man forfeited it by listening to the hissing temptations of a consummate deceiver: the Prince of Lies. Marxists think they can attain paradise through the power of totalitarian government; Judeo-Christianity teaches that paradise has been lost through disobedience of the Creator's will.

The first campaign by American Marxists on the domestic front of the Cold War they opened in the United States in the 1960s, which brought the struggle between American culture and the dogmas of Cultural Marxism home to America, was directed against U. S. military involvement in Vietnam. The attack had two purposes, the immediate purpose of suppressing support in the United States for containing communist expansion in Vietnam and, in the long-term, alienating Americans, especially young Americans, from belief in their country as an exceptional nation.

College-enrolled Americans were the most likely to be turned against their country's culture, because they were just beginning to participate in it and because they had in many cases an ingrained, middle-class respect for teachers, even those in their college classrooms and lecture halls who were doctrinaire Marxists and Marxist sympathizers. To alienate college students from the cultural beliefs of their parents and grandparents, Marxists in the 1960s invented a pair of slogans: DON'T TRUST ANYONE OVER THIRTY and QUESTION AUTHORITY. The young Americans who came of age in the Sixties and took these slogans to heart provided the Marxists their first sizeable "cadre" of college-educated, middle-class American sympathizers.

Hillary Rodham, who married the future president of the United States Bill Clinton in 1975, typifies the transformative effect Marxist indoctrinators like Saul Alinsky could have on young Americans. Alinsky (1909-1972) published his first handbook for Marxist "activism," *Reveille for Radicals*, in 1946 and in 1969, at the height of his agit-prop influence ("agit-prop" is Marxist-speak for agitation plus propaganda), *Rules for Radicals: A Practical Primer for Realistic Radicals*. Under the influence of Alinsky's hard-boiled, Marxist righteousness, Hillary Rodham was transformed from a bright, middle-class American high school student who worked in Barry Goldwater's presidential campaign to an unscrupulous "activist" in the Alinsky camp of "radicals," who arranged for her exciting new mentor to speak on her college campus. To fulfill one of her graduation requirements, Hillary Rodham wrote her senior thesis at Wellesley College in 1969 on this Marxist agitator who called himself a "community organizer." The ongoing influence of Marxists like Alinsky can be seen in the fact that two Alinskyites, Hilary Rodham Clinton and Barack Hussein Obama, contended in 2008 for the Democratic Party's nomination for the presidency of the United States. (Obama got his start in politics in 1985 by taking a teaching job at the school for training community organizers that Saul Alinsky founded in Chicago.[17])

How were such radical changes in young Americans brought about? It was done by appealing to their American cultural values and manipulating them. Take, for instance, the use PC indoctrinators in the 1960s made of American patriotism. College students then were told that real patriots were opposed to U.S. involvement in Vietnam as an unjust interference in the

---

17 David Freddon, *The Case Against Barack Obama* (Regnery, 2008), 139-143.

internal affairs of another country. They were told that the U.S. government's actions in Vietnam were imperialistic and that the people of Vietnam had as much right as the people of the thirteen colonies in 1776 to throw off the yoke of imperialism. Marxist indoctrinators on college campuses in the 1960s stressed that greed motivated U.S. policies; that American corporations were growing rich from manufacturing chemicals and bombs to maim and kill babies and other innocent people in Southeast Asia (as if Soviet and Chinese military aid to North Vietnam never caused any civilian deaths). Patriotic Americans should, therefore, take whatever steps were necessary to stop their government from aiding South Vietnam. America should let the Vietnamese settle their differences on their own. American military involvement in Southeast Asia was just prolonging the conflict.

Thus Marxist propaganda had it both ways. When the government of the United States aided and fought alongside South Vietnam military forces to repel the infiltration and invasion of South Vietnam by communist forces from North Vietnam, that was "imperialism." Soviet and Chinese aid to communist North Vietnam to overthrow South Vietnam was "liberation." It was all a matter of deceit, doctrinaire Marxist labeling, and shameless double standards.

The integrity of the vote—the essential basis for representative government—has been compromised in America by an appeal to making voter registration easier, an appeal which would surely be in America's best interest, except for the way which was devised to make it easier to register: a federal law allowing registration without having to prove U.S. citizenship. The National Voter Registration Act of 1993 (nicknamed the "Motor Voter Law") enacted by a Democratic Congress and signed into law by a Democratic president, Bill Clinton, permits persons to register to vote when obtaining a driver's license. It requires only that an applicant say he is a citizen of the United States, without having to show proof of citizenship; thus making it possible for non-citizens to vote in U.S. elections. This Act is an infringement on the U. S. Constitution because it is an illicit amendment to the Constitution (Article I, Section 2) in the guise of a federal statute.[18]

The use of one language in a country the size of Europe (Europe has 3.80 million square miles; the United States, 3.79) has been one of America's most exceptional achievements. Countless immigrants have come to America not speaking English but have adopted the language of America to avail themselves of opportunities that otherwise would have been closed to them without that ability to communicate freely. The melding of the multitude of languages the self-selected immigrants brought to America into a single language is one of the most significant meanings of the inscription *E Pluribus Unum* (Out of Many, One) on the Great Seal of the United States, and U.S. public schools were once the primary means for achieving America's exceptional unilingualism.

But the advantage of using one language in the world's third most-populous nation after China and India (Indonesia and Brazil are fourth and fifth) is being eroded by an appeal to a theory called "bilingual education," which the U.S. Department of Education is promoting. Bilingual education claims non-English-speaking students learn English better when they are instructed in their native languages. The application of the theory is undermining the acquisition of a competent level of English among students who enter U. S. public schools as speakers of a language other than English. Bilingual education is helping to make America into a multilingual nation by giving non-English

---

18 The text of the National Voter Registration Act of 1993 is available from the U. S. Department of Justice (http://www.justice.gov/crt/about/vot/42usc/subch_ih.php).

speaking immigrants and their children the idea that they have a right (the politically correct dogma of "multiculturalism") to retain their native languages and not to integrate with the rest of American society. Through its endorsement of bilingual education, the U.S. government is promoting language ghettos, where opportunities for success are more limited than in the society as a whole. Bilingual education is reversing America's exceptional history of unilingualism and cultural assimilation by appealing to compassion for non-English speaking students.

Political Correctness, which has made bilingual education one of its dogmas, has also undermined American cultural unity through its successful campaign to remove signs of respect for belief in God from U.S. public schools, thus weakening the foundation of America's culture (see Appendix B, The Argument in the Declaration of Independence). In the 1960s, by invoking "freedom of religion," a series of lawsuits were filed in State courts, lost, and were appealed up to the U.S. Supreme Court. These suits demanded that exercises in prayer and Bible reading at the beginning of a school day and the display of the Ten Commandments at public schools be declared unconstitutional. The Supreme Court went along with these demands and prohibited such exercises and displays as "unconstitutional" violations of an alleged right not to be offended by expressions of religious sentiments which differ from one's own religious sentiments, including the protection of the religious sentiments of atheists, who were plaintiffs in several of the suits. These successes bolstering the leading dogma of Cultural Marxism—that material reality is the only reality—were achieved *in the name of freedom of religion.* Granting constitutional status to a bogus, un-American right not to be offended by expressions of belief in God in the public schools cancels the American belief that no one conducting himself in "a peaceable and orderly manner, shall ever be molested on account of his mode of worship or religious sentiments" (Article 1, Northwest Ordinance). In the name of upholding freedom of religion, the Supreme Court has suppressed the free exercise of religion. It has endorsed the bizarre proposition that reverence for God and his laws historically expressed in the Declaration of Independence, Washington's "Farewell Address," the Northwest Ordinance, and other state papers and throughout the history of public school education in America is antithetical to religious freedom. Moreover, the Supreme Court has amended the Constitution of the United States by usurping jurisdiction over religion.

The Court's rulings protecting anyone from hearing or seeing signs of belief in God and his Ten Commandments in U. S. public schools were, in effect, bans on teaching respect for the Judeo-Christian moral tradition, particularly respect for other human beings and the sanctity of human life. Changes in student behavior soon followed: unprecedented classroom violence, including assaults on teachers, and vandalism to school property—assaults and vandalism so acute that some school districts hired uniformed guards in an effort to reduce their occurrence; an unprecedented increase in cheating;[19] an unprecedented increase in sexual activity that saw a 700 percent rise in teenage pregnancies[20] and a need for classes to accommodate pregnant female students; and following the federal judiciary's bans on prayer, Bible reading, and displays of the Ten Commandments at public schools, some of those schools experienced premeditated murders which have come to be blandly referred as "school shootings," as if the availability of guns rather than disrespect for human life and Judeo-Christian standards for moral conduct, was the root cause of such killings. (It must be noted in this

---

19 For a study of this phenomenon, see Daniel R. Levine, "Cheating in Schools: A National Scandal." *Reader's Digest*, October 1996, 66-67.
20 David Barton, *Separation of Church and State: What the Founders Meant* (Wallbuilder, 2007), 17.

regard that at private schools where federal judges have not claimed religious jurisdiction and banned signs of respect for God and his laws, there have been no "school shootings.")

The occurrence of one or two of these behavioral changes after the Supreme Court's bans on signs of respect for belief in God and his laws in America's public schools might be dismissed as just coincidence. But not *five* changes: marked increases in violence to persons, violence to property, academic cheating, and sexual activity, and unprecedented murders on school grounds. Five such changes in the behavior of public school students following the Supreme Court bans on expressions of belief in God at public schools suggests a causal connection to the Court's prohibitions.

The Supreme Court has also been manipulated to devalue human life in another way by another appeal to the American cultural belief in freedom.

Common sense and Judeo-Christian teaching concur that an abortion is the taking of a human life in development, which is why every State in the Union prior to 1973 had statutes which either prohibited or restricted abortions. "Abortion rights" were a priority of Political Correctness from the movement's inception; and in *Roe v. Wade*, 410 U. S. 113 (1973), the U. S. Supreme Court was persuaded to make abortion a constitutional right. In that 1973 case, the argument for "abortion rights" held that since freedom requires choice, a pregnant woman must be allowed the choice of terminating the human life developing in her body. If that was not constitutionally allowed, the Supreme Court of the United States would be enslaving women to the State statutes that compelled her to bear and give birth to a human being. This argument transformed abortion from the destruction of a human life into "the right to choose" to destroy a human life. What is chosen no longer matters. All that matters is "the right to choose." "Abortion rights" claims abortion is *not* the destruction of a human life because human zygotes, embryos, and fetuses are not human beings. But isn't the purpose of abortion to prevent the birth of a human baby and all that entails? The life being snuffed out and the physical trauma and psychological risks for the women undergoing an abortion are not issues for "abortion rights" advocates. The only issue for them is the right to choose to destroy a human being at any stage of its development, even during the parturition of a full-term, viable baby emerging from the mother's body because, technically, the baby has yet to become independent of the mother's body. The RIGHT TO CHOOSE is now the most dogmatic slogan of Political Correctness besides SEPARATION OF CHURCH AND STATE. Both of these slogans sound wonderfully American, and the tens of millions of abortion in the United States since 1973 attest to the devaluation of human life which has occurred in America because of the RIGHT TO CHOOSE in the name of freedom.

Judeo-Christian marriage has been another object of PC attack using a value of American culture as the weapon of attack, this time equality rather than freedom. The Judeo-Christian teaching that marriage is *the union for life* (in every sense of "for life") of one man and one woman has been fundamental to Western civilization and is now being debased by claiming that two male or two female homosexuals (the term applies to both genders) have the "right to marry." Western civilization's most fundamental social institution (marriage) is being redefined by PC homosexuals who claim they are no different from heterosexual couples when it comes to marriage, though marriage is society's age-old institution for natural procreation and the rearing of children by both natural parents: a definition that disqualifies homosexuals from alleging any right to marry. The argument that homosexuals are being deprived of a "right to marry" must be examined in light of the fact that they cannot fulfill the intended purpose of the institution of marriage. Neither does the argument that homosexuals are just like other folks when it comes to marriage square with the insistence of homosexuals in vaunting their "sexual orientation" that they are *different* from other human beings and proud of it. Can it be unjust to take notice in law of something members of a group insist on and take pride in? The recognition in law of a difference in the physical coupling of human beings should not be regarded as unjust by those who take pride in their peculiar coupling, which prevents them from ever being natural parents.

The retort of apologists for "same-sex marriage" that not all marriages between a man and a woman lead to natural birth is of course a matter of fact observation. But the observation does not address the defining intention of the ancient institution of marriage underlying Western society, which is to produce children from the union of one man and one woman in marriage and to have the parents of those children raise them.

One might also ask in regard to the oxymoronic idea of "same-sex marriage," how is it that the federal government claims jurisdiction over marriage when the Tenth Amendment so plainly states: "The powers not delegated to the United States by the Constitution, nor prohibited by it to the States, are reserved to the States respectively, or to the people" and the Constitution of the United States makes no explicit or implied grant of such authority to the federal government? To allow federal judges to say what marriage is, is to condone the usurpation of a power the Constitution clearly reserves to the jurisdiction of the States and their statutes and courts.

Appealing to the Constitution, to equality, to freedom, to ease in registering to vote, to allegedly better education practices, and to other basics of American culture has been the principal tactic of Politically Correct "activists" in prosecuting their intention to transform America's culture. Americans are being lured into doing what Abraham Lincoln warned against: committing national suicide.

The tactic has been most effective in federal courts, including the Supreme Court, because federal judges can be tempted to overstep the bounds of their constitutional limits when offered the opportunity to enlarge their jurisdiction, if they are persuaded that their exercise of illicit judicial authority will serve some basic American value such as freedom, equality, or education. Every American of intelligence and goodwill reveres the U.S. Constitution as indispensable to the unity of the United States. They are therefore inclined to accept a ruling by the Supreme Court, even when they sense it is harmful to America's culture and even contrary to some plain meaning of the Constitution. The general reverence of Americans for the Constitution is what makes appeals to constitutionality by PC activists so effective. Such appeals to what Americans hold dear is the primary means by which American culture is being fundamentally "changed" (i.e. transformed). The technique is similar to that of jujitsu: leverage the opponent's strength against him to overthrow him.

Were the people of the United States better versed in the requirements of the Constitution they revere (especially Article V, the Bill of Rights, and the Fourteenth Amendment), they would put a stop to the Supreme Court's usurpation of power over such matters as abortion, education, marriage, and religion, especially the Court's so-called "Incorporation Doctrine," which contends that the Fourteenth Amendment gave the federal government protective jurisdiction over the rights of every American enumerated in the Bill of Rights.

To make their illicit amendments to the Constitution, federal judges have had to ignore the Ninth and the Tenth Amendments. In doing that, they violate their oath of office to uphold the Constitution of the United States: not just some of its requirements.

To convince themselves that the Ninth and Tenth Amendments can be judicially ignored, judges must believe that serving some interest greater than the Constitution justifies ignoring parts of the Constitution. The truth of the matter is that there can be no graver danger to the interest the people of the States have in liberty under law than judges who think they have the authority to decide which parts of the laws entrusted to their care may be overlooked. No judge, whether federal or State, in making his judgments may legitimately ignore any part of the Constitution of the United States, the only American law the people of all the States have approved. Judges who think they can amend the Constitution under color of interpreting it are placing themselves above the Constitution and disgracing their office.

But the *high crime* of trashing the Constitution is not being committed only by federal judges (Article II, Section 4, declares: "The President, Vice-President and all civil Officers of the United States, shall be removed from Office on Impeachment for, and Conviction of, Treason, Bribery, and other *high Crimes and Misdemeanors*," italics added). The executive and the legislative branches of the general government have also been guilty of ignoring the Ninth and the Tenth Amendments. It's simply easier for PC activists to influence courts to create false readings of the Constitution and exercise powers not granted them under the Constitution because judicial decisions are made by one judge or a small number of judges (in the case of the Supreme Court five) rather than by a legislative majority. The same is true of the executive branch: only one person has to be influenced.

The Tenth Amendment was expressly written to prohibit unwarranted expansions of federal jurisdiction. This part of the Constitution cannot be repeated too often or too emphatically: "*The powers not delegated to the United States by the Constitution, nor prohibited by it to the States, are reserved to the States respectively, or to the people.*" The Tenth Amendment gives the States exclusive authority over abortion, marriage, public schools, and religion, since nowhere in the Constitution is jurisdiction over these matters delegated to the general government. By trespassing on the States' sole constitutional jurisdiction in these and other matters, the federal judiciary has tremendously weakened the chief means for keeping the federal government within its proper constitutional limits: namely the division of federal from State jurisdiction. The adjective "supreme" in the Supreme Court's name (Article III, Section 1) does not give it authority in all cases whatsoever. The framers of the Constitution expected the judicial branch of the general government to operate within the constraints of the Constitution, the same as the other two branches. Politically correct activists, however, want the Supreme Court to have authority in all cases whatsoever, because that suits their intention to overturn America's lawful government and replace it with a politically correct dictatorship.

Now that officers in the federal government are usurping and exercising powers the Constitution reserves to the States and the people of the States, the time has come to invoke the provision in Article V by which the States can *propose* as well as ratify amendments. The right of the States to do that must be exercised to return the federal government to proper subservience to the Constitution after many decades of exceeding its constitutional authority, a situation reminiscent of that described in the Declaration of Independence in regard to the British government in 1757-1775. The power of the States to propose as well as ratify amendments needs to be exercised for the good of the Union.

A Bill of Restrictions containing a set of amendments is needed because a single amendment could not rein in the now totally out of control federal government. The Bill might include, for instance, an amendment to change Article I, Section 6, on how congressmen are compensated, and require each State to determine by law and pay from its State treasury the salaries and benefits of its congressional delegation; thus making every member of Congress aware in a substantial way that they are the paid servants of the people of the States who elect them. (At present, Congress decides its own pay and benefits and appropriates the money from the U.S. Treasury.) The Bill of Restrictions might also grant the States a power to impeach and try any officer in the federal government for the high crime of violating a requirement of the Constitution: the fifty State chief justices to bring the impeachment and the fifty State governors to try it, a two-thirds majority being needed in both instances to complete the process of removing a federal official from office for disobeying the Constitution. The lead amendment in the Bill of Restrictions should be a declaration that the twenty-six personal rights and liberties enumerated in the first eight articles of amendment to the Constitution are under the exclusive jurisdiction of the States.

Ever since Franklin Roosevelt's aptly named "New Deal" presidency of 1933-1945, the three branches of the federal government have increasingly been exercising powers not granted to them in the Constitution. Each of these usurpations has been an unwarranted amendment to the Constitution. A Bill of Restrictions proposed and ratified by the people of the States would nullify powers usurped by the federal government and restore the sovereign control of the people of the States over their general government.

Three trends in the behavior of the U.S. government have become quite evident since 1933. (1) The constitutional principle of a separation of powers between the federal government and the States and among the three branches of the general government is no longer being observed by the U.S. government. Particularly troublesome has been Congress's numerous transfers to executive branch agencies it has created (the Department of Health and Human Services, the Department of Education, the Environmental Protection Agency, etc.) of authority to make "regulations" which have for the people of the States the force of laws enacted in accordance with Article I, Section 7 of the Constitution. These transfers of legislative authority to executive branch agencies directly violate Article I, Section 1 of the Constitution. "All legislative Powers herein granted shall be vested in a Congress of the United States, which shall consist of a Senate and House of Representatives." The head of the executive branch, the President of the United States, has likewise been exercising unconstitutional authority in issuing decrees called "executive orders" that the people of the States must obey as if they were laws. The president is also exercising an unconstitutional absolute veto over all federal legislation by deciding which laws or parts of laws enacted by Congress and signed by previous presidents he personally deems worthy of enforcement. (2) An inordinate amount of power has been concentrated in the executive branch of the government with the approval, either passive or active, of one or both of the government's other branches. Congress has been culpable for much of this concentration of power by unconstitutionally delegating to executive-branch agencies, in defiance of Article I, Sections 1 and 7, its responsibility to exercise the legislative power of the general government. (3) The judicial branch of the government has amended the Constitution under color of interpreting it.

The cumulative effect of these three trends has been an almost complete cancellation of the Separation of Powers principle, thus a structural weakening of the ratified Constitution embodying the sovereign will of the people of the States.

Increasingly in the last half-century, government in the United States has been conducted as if federal jurisdiction were the only jurisdiction in America. Increasingly, the States have been reduced to the status of administrative units of the federal government. Increasingly the administration of the federal government has moved away from the concept of a government of laws (allegiance to which is the basis for government in the United States) toward a government which serves the special interest of staying in office of the persons who administer the government rather than serving the general interest of the people of the States in liberty under law through obedience to the Constitution of the United States. The defining duty of every member of the U.S. government is obedience to the Constitution. All else is secondary to that imperative.

Since the three branches of the general government are not inclined to put a stop to these trends and return the government to subservience to the Constitution, the intervention of the sovereign power of the people of the States must be exerted.

The unconstitutional trends in the administration of the federal government have manifested themselves in the government's reckless spending of more than it takes in. In 1930, three years prior to "the New Deal," the share of the national debt which every man, woman, and child in America owed was $131. Today that per capita share of the national debt exceeds $50,000 because since the end of World War II in 1945, there have been 58 years of deficit spending (borrowing to make up the difference between government expenditures and revenues) and only 12 years in which the U.S. government spent less than it took in.[21]

The general government's lopsided deficit spending since World War II (five years of deficit spending for every year of balanced budgets) is a prescription for a fiscal calamity that can only be avoided by reducing the U.S. government's expenditures to less than its revenues and paying down the current astronomical national debt of trillions of dollars. If this is not done, even the largest national economy the world has ever seen may not recover from the disaster. Unless the U. S. government's

---

21 "Federal Receipts, Outlays, and Surpluses or Deficits, 1901-2014," *The World Almanac and Book of Facts 2015*, 67.

borrowing of tremendous sums of money to support deficit spending is stopped, the American way of life will be destroyed, as future generations of Americans are forced to spend more and more of their earnings to pay the interest on the overwhelming national debt they have inherited from the spendthrift habits of today's general government.

The new language Political Correctness has created in America since the 1960s has enabled the movement's attacks on America's culture which, in the name of improving America, are creating behaviors that are destroying it.

Language is always undergoing piecemeal, natural changes through the spontaneous usages of its speakers and writers. The changes Political Correctness has been making to American speech have not been like that. They have been deliberate, not spontaneous. They have been programmatic changes to America's vocabulary for the purpose of changing the perceptions of Americans. Relentless sloganeering has accompanied these changes to pound the new vocabulary into the minds of Americans, and slander is used to discredit whoever denounces the new-speak and its perceptions. Such Americans are attacked as "racists," "sexists," "homophobes," "bigots," and "facists."

Here is a sampling of some of the new terms Political Correctness has coined for its purposes: African American, animal rights, bilingual education, Christian extremism, consciousness raising, entitlement, environmentalism, feminism, hate speech, Hispanic, homelessness, homophobia, Islamophobia, lifestyle, male chauvinism, multiculturalism, Native American, no-fault divorce, nonjudgmental, racial profiling, right-wing extremism, same-sex marriage, sensitivity training, sexism, sexual harassment, single parenting, underprivileged, victimization. The new lexicon of Political Correctness is far more extensive than this sampling.

At the same time Political Correctness has been inventing new terms, it has also been censoring old ones. For instance, the use of *man* to mean any human being—a usage as old as recorded English—has been forbidden as offensive to women. The use of *man* has been prohibited in regard to women even as a syllable, as, for example, *chairman* (any person heading an organization), *flagman* (any person controlling traffic at a highway construction site), and *congressman* (any person elected to Congress). None of these terms, and many others having the suffix *man,* was intended to be gender-specific, though when they came into use there may have been few female chairmen and no female flagmen or congressmen. Not until Political Correctness came along were such words censored.

To be Politically Correct today, references to a woman must be either gender-neutral coinages such as "chair" and "flagperson" or female-specific coinages like "congresswoman." PC speech is well illustrated in the diction of a longtime college dean in his fiftieth undergraduate reunion yearbook entry telling of interviewing applicants to his alma mater: "Of those I have interviewed in the past few years, one is now a happy Princeton freshperson, another a sophomore..."[22]

Henry Beard's and Christopher Cerf's sardonic *Official Politically Correct Dictionary and Handbook* (Villard Books, 1992) provides an overview of politically correct speech, which includes numerous PC coinages to avoid the generic suffix man when referring to females. (Try as they might, and they have tried, PC activists have been unable to dislodge the word *woman* from American speech which contains the hated suffix *man.*) *The New Thought Police* by Tammy Bruce (Forum, 2001) and *The Language Police* by Diane Ravitch (Knopf, 2003) are other informative works on PC language activism.

---

22 The entry for William F. Halloran, PhD, in *Princeton University Class of 1956: 50th Reunion* (June, 2006), 168.

The words *housewife* and *homemaker* are among the terms that have been censored by Political Correctness. In this instance, the censorship was achieved through massive propaganda associating the words with demeaning drudgery, "male dominance," a constricted "lifestyle," and even slavery. Nowadays the once honorable female vocations of being a housewife or a homemaker, which politically correct women are supposed to shun, are now considered so horrific they are unmentionable. Nowadays, because of PC censorship, these once common but now despised words are seldom encountered outside the obituaries of elderly women.

Politically correct activists routinely control language and hence perceptions by accusing their opponents of being and doing what they themselves are and do. Such preemptive accusations shield Political Correctness from the criticism it deserves to have. The tactic of preemptive accusation is effective because a critic of Political Correctness would appear childish if, after being accused of doing or being something PC activists either do or are, he then accused his accuser of that same thing. Politically correct activists by accusing opponents of, say, intolerance, racism, or "hate speech" avoid being called intolerant, racist, and hateful, which they most certainly are. Other preemptive, protective accusations are "bullying" and the "imposition" of Christian morality. The exact opposite is true. Political Correctness is being imposed, and PC activists are the biggest of all bullies. Christian morality was firmly in place in America long before the politically correct movement started. PC dogmatism is what is being imposed on everyone today, and politically correct bullying is pervasive in American institutions.

Redefining words is another feature of PC language activism. The terms *extreme* and *extremism*, for example, now designate whoever and whatever PC activists have targeted for elimination. *Controversial* is another label for someone or something PC activists want to get rid of, regardless of whether the activity, idea, or person so labeled has in fact lots of public support. (Whatever is labeled "controversial" automatically becomes questionable.) *Discrimination*, which once meant making careful, analytic distinctions, has been revamped to mean the manifestation of a prejudice. (The sloganeering and name-calling which are inherent to PC propaganda are the exact opposite of discriminating in the old meaning of the word.) *Diversity* now means forced college and university admissions and forced employment of "underrepresented classes." *Equality*, which before the PC movement meant having the same God-given birthrights as other human beings, now means giving "the underprivileged" special class privileges. The word *secular*, which once designated something non-religious, has been redefined to mean the suppression of religion and is for politically correct writers and speakers the preferred euphemism for atheism.

Before Political Correctness, the term *budget cut* meant reducing funding for a federal program, but in the 1990s it was redefined to mean an increase in funding that was below the previous rate of increase. (If, say, the previous rate of increase had been 5 percent and the next increase in a program's budget was only 3 percent, that was, in PC-speak, a "budget cut.") *Education* K through 12 no longer means guiding American children and adolescents through the process of *getting* the knowledge, skills, and moral values that will enable them to make their way in the world independent of government handouts. The PC definition of education is *giving* children and adolescents (and "college kids") "the education they deserve," i.e. indoctrinating them in Political Correctness.

Much of the teaching in America's public schools today is devoted to "self-esteem" which substitutes the secular cliché "You're special" for the Judeo-Christian doctrine "You're God's creation." (Which of these pronouncements: you're "special" or you're "God's creation," do you think is more conducive to enduring self-esteem?) Telling students they're "special," which is replacing teaching them that they are a creation of God, is discouraging the individual competitiveness inherent to America's achievement-oriented culture. "Self-esteem" is based on the "secular" dogma that human life does not come from God and teaches students they don't have to use their God-given talents to the utmost to gain the esteem of others. PC indoctrination is getting kids to think of themselves as winners deserving of awards and accolades without having to win.

The most fundamental change in perception, however, through the introduction of PC language in America has been in regard to class consciousness.

Before the domestic front in the USSR-USA Cold War was opened in the United States in the 1960s, Americans used to boast that they lived in "a classless society." By that they meant, of course, that American society is not based on a belief in a fixed birth status but rather on the conviction that a person born into a lower social class can rise to a higher social rank through individual striving and accomplishment. The emphasis America's culture puts on success and upward mobility, in combination with the abundance of opportunities the self-selected immigrants and their descendants found in America, has created the world's largest middle class in the United States.

Marx's allegedly scientific analysis of history proposes a different concept of progress, based on *class* struggle. It calls for the working class to rise *en mass* and replace "the ruling class," the "exploiters" who are oppressing mankind. This revolution will be led, of course, by doctrinaire Marxists: the intellectual "vanguard" of the uprising to liberate the world's masses from the chains of capitalism, today's form of oppression. In the Marxist view of human history, the belief that the Creator of the universe has given human beings freedom to pursue and achieve happiness through individual effort is absurd because God does not exist. And as long as belief in self-determination prevailed in America, the chances of a Marxist revolution in the United States were next to zero. Belief in self-determination had to be eliminated and something useful to class struggle put in its place. Biology provided that something.

Biology has naturally always been part of personal identity. But by incessantly harping only on race, gender, ethnicity, and "sexual orientation" and classifying persons according to their birth in one of those biological categories and making that the only basis of identity, Political Correctness has created a new consciousness that is primarily a consciousness of birth-class. The biologically-fixed categories of race, gender, ethnicity, and "sexual orientation" are replacing the American idea of class as primarily a matter of wealth, which can be regarded as self-determining. Biology is the new "identity politics" in America.

Biological class consciousness is well-suited to the Marxian doctrine of class struggle because almost no one can change their biology, which according to PC dogma includes "sexual orientation." In this scheme of things, there can be little ambiguity about anyone's class identity. Either one is a "victimizer" (i.e. an oppressor, a straight white male) or a "victim," (a member of one of the oppressed classes: women, blacks, "ethnics," and homosexuals which are deserving of special privileges and government protection).

Consequently, since biology is a given, changing biological victimization requires a revolutionary cultural transformation in order to bring "social justice" to the oppressed. (The idea of "social justice" is justice for *classes* of persons, not for individuals.) For anyone who subscribes to the new biological class consciousness, belief in improving one's social status through individual effort is stupid. Only *class struggle* and the creation of an all-controlling government to achieve "social justice" can improve the lives of biologically "victimized" classes. When oppression is a matter of "racism," "sexism," "homophobia," and "bigotry," a complete cultural transformation and total government control is called for to correct that injustice.

Biological class consciousness is a regression to the European idea of birth-classes. During the Russian Revolution of 1917, Marxists used the slogan ALL POWER TO THE SOVIETS to arouse the masses to action. The comparable call for social justice in the United States is EMPOWER MINORITIES. And for the purpose of Marxist revolution, American women, who have long comprised more than half the U.S. population,[23] have been redefined as a "minority." This has been necessary because in a revolution no one sympathizes with the majority. To forward Marxist class struggle in America, the biological majority had to be redefined and perceived as a minority.

Indoctrinating Americans to think in terms of biological classes has been institutionalized through courses and degree programs at American colleges and universities in "African-American Studies," "Feminist Studies," "Mexican-American Studies," "Native American Studies," so-called "Queer Studies" (i.e. homosexuality), and other biologically-defined groups. Biological class consciousness is now part of every level of education in America. Even kindergarteners have stories read to them of families with "two mommies."

The PC dogma of "diversity" is part of this biological class consciousness, and it has become a goal embraced by American professional schools, the federal government, and business corporations. Every large corporation and every reputable institution of higher learning in the United States has an Office of Diversity charged with overseeing publicity on "diversity" and arranging

---

23 *Historical Statistics of the United States Colonial Times to 1970* (U.S. Department of Commerce, Bureau of the Census, 1989), Part 1, Series A23-26, 9. *The World Almanac and Book of Facts 2015*, 617.

lectures, workshops, and seminars for disseminating and promoting the concept. It's the thing to do. U.S. corporations currently employ thousands of full time indoctrinators to teach the need for diversity, what it means, and how to attain it. This PC dogma is creating the conviction that being part of a "victimized" biological class has economic value. It "entitles" (as PC-speakers like to have everybody say) members of an oppressed biological class to a job with good pay and good benefits. These days, what happened, or presumably happened, to at least some of a person's biological ancestors is more relevant than a person's productivity and ability to contribute to the success of an enterprise. The future-orientation of American culture is being lost. The hope of individual success is being replaced by an entitlement mentality based on events in the ancestral past. No more, "it's up to you to get ahead and excel in life." The paranoia of being kept down by oppressors is the dominant idea today.

Because class consciousness today in America is mainly a matter of color, gender, "sexual orientation," and ethnicity, belief in the freedom of individuals to be upwardly mobile through their own efforts is diminishing and belief in "social justice" is on the rise. The current prevalence of biological class consciousness makes belief in a society without fixed birth-classes difficult to comprehend. Marx's "scientific" analysis of history precludes the possibility of an exceptional society, because to do science requires that everything, everywhere always works the same way, which means in regard to Marxist dogma that everything operates in accordance with materialistic determinism. If you're born oppressed, you remain oppressed until the social, political, and physical environment is improved through revolutionary governmental interventions. Martin Luther King's vision of a racially-integrated society of upwardly mobile white Americans and upwardly mobile black Americans, who, he said, only needed an equal opportunity to be self-determining, is the antithesis of

Marxism. The philosophy of materialistic determinism which animates Marxism denies the existence of freewill, even though Marxists are extremely willful in their attempts to impose their views on non-believers in materialistic determinism.

Decades of PC agit-prop in America promoting biological class consciousness as a precondition for revolution make it possible to claim that no matter how powerful a black American may actually be, that he is still a "victim" of racism. According to Political Correctness, racism still abounds in America and is operating to the detriment of the black American who has been elected to the presidency of the United States twice.

Political Correctness which includes the dogmas that whites victimize blacks, men victimize women, and the majority of Americans victimize homosexual and ethnic minorities claims that no member of an oppressed or "victimized" biological class is capable of racism, sexism, homophobia, or bigotry. This Marxian class mentality exculpates "minorities" of class wrongdoing which only straight white males are (theoretically) capable of and is changing the feelings of many respectable, middle-class Americans about their country. Political Correctness wants Americans to think that America has never been a land of opportunity but has always been, and remains, a land of oppression which must be "fundamentally transformed."

Recently, one PC agit-prop campaign created a hullabaloo in the media that "1 percent" of American society was oppressing the other "99 percent" (as if America's immense middle class did not exist). This claim could not be more Marxist or more preposterous. To believe that a ratio of oppressors to oppressed of 1 to 99 exists in America requires accepting the lie that millions of Americans earning $100,000 or more a year are "oppressed." This propaganda event was so preposterous that it makes one wonder whether it might have been a PC trial balloon to test how many American Leftists would actually accept these slogans about "the 1 percent" and "the 99 percent" that they were being fed and would act on them. In this case, the action they were told to take was to "occupy" particular areas of America's cities to protest against the oppression of "the 99 percent" by "the 1 percent." That a conspiracy of such enormity could exist is typical of the persecution complex (paranoia) that permeates Marxist thought.

The notion that a person's life is determined by the oppression one's ancestors suffered is the principal Marxist dogma regarding America's history. (If this were true, how is it that so many self-selected immigrants from Europe's lower classes improved their lives in America?) The idea that the oppression one's biological ancestors suffered in the past determines a person's life in the present absolves individuals of responsibility for failure and transfers it to "society." In this Marxist myth, every failure is traceable to "racism," "sexism," "homophobia," and "bigotry" because to doctrinaire Marxists, wrongdoing is class-specific rather than an inherent potential of human freedom. Thus many black, female, homosexual, and ethnic Americans today, no matter how well-off they may be, believe straight white males as a class are oppressing them. Many straight white males, having been accused for decades of being oppressors, now make a point of behaving and speaking in politically correct ways to avoid such slander. The federal government is playing a major role in the Marxist campaign to portray America as a land of oppression. It has been persuaded to act as if it exists primarily to implement "social justice," establish "compassion," and distribute "entitlements."

Americans today are being conditioned to feel that federal handouts are essential to leading a decent life. In Marxist theory, wealth is *not* the result of the inventiveness, hard work, and responsible, entrepreneurial behavior of individuals but rather is a social construct to which "the disadvantaged" are "entitled" to share. Wealth in this view is a product of society. No individual builds or creates anything. "Society" builds it, and for any class to be outstandingly rich is a misdistribution of what society has created. Sadly, even a U.S. senator from Massachusetts (Elizabeth Warren) and the current president of the United States (Barack Hussein Obama) have publicly endorsed this Marxist theory of how wealth is created. Cultural Marxism promises happiness, not the pursuit of it. PC agit-prop is deconstructing American individualism and imposing socialist thinking and is making more and more Americans feel that comprehensive government control benefits everyone.

Political Correctness has planted new ways of thinking in the minds of tens of millions of Americans through its new-speak perceptions, its biological class consciousness, its indoctrination of students K through PhD, its domination of the media, and its manipulation of the values of America's culture and middle-class American virtues such as compassion, fairness, tolerance, and politeness (the avoidance of giving offense). A society in which the majority once ruled is becoming a society ruled by minorities "empowered" by Political Correctness. Increasingly, American society is becoming a collection of aggrieved biological "minorities" motivated not by the freedom to imagine opportunities and the urge to fulfill them, but by a concern with biological class consciousness, obsession with the ancestral past, and "social justice."

The U.S. government is funding this deconstruction of America's culture. Congress's constitutional power to borrow money (Article I, Section 8, Clause 2) is paying for the plethora of "programs" that promote the idea of class justice through Big Government. Nearly half of every dollar now being spent by the national government is borrowed. The idea of a "debt limit" has no meaning when Congress continually increases the limit so it can borrow and spend more money. The special interest of politicians of staying in office is served by this borrow-and-spend conduct that is annually distributing trillions of dollars borrowed on the credit of the people of the States, loans which future generations of Americans will have to pay the interest on without themselves having benefited from the borrowed money. (Is this fair?) Voters today would never tolerate the current level of federal spending if they had to pay for it from their taxes. Massive borrowing is another matter. Politicians are accustoming taxpayers to government subsidies without worrying about the massive borrowing which funds them. Future generations will take care of that. America's culture heretofore has been future oriented. But the well-being of future generations no longer seems to matter. What matters is Marxian "social justice" in the here and now, whatever it costs.

Perhaps 15 percent of the American public today is firmly in the camp of Political Correctness. Another segment of the public of indeterminate and fluctuating size has been indoctrinated to go along with the hostile dogmas of Political Correctness and has become comparatively indifferent to America's future. Consequently, the threat of a fullblown Marxist government in America is continuing to increase. Too many young Americans are graduating from high school and college ignorant of the exceptional nature of America's culture and lacking the knowledge, skills, and moral values to succeed on their own, but brimming over with belief in "self-esteem," "diversity," "victimization," "social justice," "racism," "multiculturalism," and "environmentalism." Moreover, many older middle-class Americans who know from personal experience and foreign travel that America's culture is exceptional have lost confidence in America, it seems, and can be heard saying they fear for the future of their children and grandchildren and are glad they won't be around to see it.

There are good reasons, however, for believing American culture will not succumb to Political Correctness. For one thing, cultural beliefs, the historical beliefs that take over four generations to become cultural beliefs, are extraordinarily resilient.

We should also remember, despite the seeming invincibility of Political Correctness, that few persons in the United States foresaw the collapse of the USSR twenty-five years ago. The continuance of the Soviet Union after World War II seemed absolutely assured. But it wasn't. Almost alone, an American president with a firm faith in America's future spoke for the peoples under Soviet rule in Central Europe (the Poles, the east Germans, the Hungarians, the Czechs, the Slovaks) in calling the Soviet Union "an evil empire." And by predicting that the Marxist regime in Russia was in its last days, he raised their hopes. But up to the moment that the USSR actually collapsed in 1989-1991 practically everyone else in America accepted the Soviet line that it was a "superpower." A similar total collapse of Political Correctness seems to be in the offing.

Although the agit-prop of Political Correctness which is undermining America's culture has turned the thinking of tens of millions of Americans against their country and conditioned many others to be indifferent to its future, the Americans who love their country and feel it is exceptional, and are grateful to be an American, still far outnumbers those Americans who have accepted the Marxist line that the United States has been and is a cesspool of economic exploitation, social oppression, racism, sexism, homophobia, and bigotry which deserves to have its high opinion of itself knocked down.

Besides the majority of Americans who continue to believe in God and are grateful to be Americans, a further reason for hope exists in the fact that the people of the States have proven their courage, resourcefulness, and devotion to freedom on many previous occasions when faced with serious challenges. And these traits of America's culture will be needed to meet the danger which Political Correctness poses. The techniques

American Marxists have been employing to "deconstruct" America's culture have succeeded to the extent that they have only because too few Americans have taken Political Correctness seriously as the threat to the American way of life that it is. Once enough Americans understand the techniques of Political Correctness, the people of the States will come up with ways to roll back PC propaganda. Once Americans understand that today's skyrocketing national debt is a strategy for destroying America, they will cease their complacency about and complicity in the government's profligate borrowing and spending and put a stop to it. The generations now alive in the United States are still the sons and daughters of liberty when they understand their country is in danger.

Perhaps the best reason for hope, however, lies in remembering what happened behind the Iron Curtain in the 1980s. For no matter how bad things may seem to be in America today, they are not as bad as they were in the colonies the Soviet Union established in Central Europe in Poland, eastern Germany, Hungary, and what is now the Czech Republic and Slovakia after World War II. (The Soviet Union mounted a highly successful propaganda to get Westerners to refer to these countries in Central Europe as "Eastern Europe" to mask its penetration into Central Europe: Eastern Europe being in the Soviets' "sphere of influence." But the truth is the truth; and the border between West and East Germany which marked the extent of Soviet imperialism in Central Europe was 1,150 miles from Moscow but only 420 miles from London.) The obedient communist parties the USSR installed in Central Europe, like the Soviet government itself, totally controlled each colony's agriculture, commerce, communications, education, entertainment, healthcare, jobs, housing, journalism, justice, laws, manufacturing, media, police, politics, prices, transportation, travel, and wages.

Only those who have lived under communist government

can appreciate the difference between what Marxism claims to be and what it truly is. The chronic shortages of food, medicine, electricity, soap, toilet paper, and other staples and amenities of modern life; the shoddy work standards in a society whose government denies the value of private property ("We pretend to work and they pretend to pay us"). The long hours standing in line every day trying to buy whatever may be available in a store or a shop to barter later with friends and acquaintances (other deprived consumers) for what each person really needs. The lies and half-truths on television and in the press about how well the economy is doing; the constant self-censorship which prevents people from speaking the truth with complete candor on the job, at school, or in the marketplace (you never know who might be listening and report you to the Party for speaking the truth). The anxiety that you might offend someone in authority (toe the mark the Party sets or you risk losing your job, your daughter is not admitted to college, or your family is not assigned the slightly-bigger apartment you applied for years ago). Then, too, there's the "telephone justice," whereby a Party official phones a judge to tell him the verdict he will hand down in a trial and the one-candidate-per-office "elections." Voting in these one-party charades called elections is mandatory in communist regimes. It is officially called "participatory democracy." By making adult human beings "elect" one nominee per office (the Party's nominee) conditions them to do whatever they are told to do.

That was life in communist-ruled Poland and the other Soviet-controlled colonies in Central Europe. That is life today in communist-ruled Cuba and every country with a government based on Marxism's one-party tyranny.

Nonetheless, a freedom movement called *Solidarnosć* (Solidarity) was organized in Poland. It took the form of a popular Christian labor union, which had its impetus in 1978 when a Polish cardinal was elected by his fellow cardinals to head the

THE PARAMOUNT DANGER TO AMERICA

Roman Catholic Church, the first non-Italian pontiff in five centuries. The next year, Pope John Paul II visited his native Poland and preached a series of powerful sermons to immense open-air congregations. He told his compatriots they must not be afraid. They needed to be brave, he said, and to never forget they were children of God. He told them that human life is sacred. He told them to love God and trust in him and to use the gifts of reason and freedom God had given them to do what was right. He preached the nobility of man and the dignity of human labor. He preached the need for Christian marriage. He aroused the people of Poland from their torpor of living under Marxist rule. He spoke God's truth and inspired them with his love of God. As one university student who made a pilgrimage with some of her classmates to be with John Paul at a rural shrine told me, "There we were, thousands of us, silently praying with the Holy Father, and you could feel the power rising up through the trees."

After the Polish Pope returned to Rome, Solidarity was born; and a 39-year-old shipyard electrician named Lech Walesa was elected president of this unique labor union. Never in the history of organized labor has there ever been a national labor union like Solidarity. Persons from every trade and occupation belonged. To join, you only had to be Polish, employed, able to pay ten dollars in annual dues, and brave enough to do something you knew the Party wouldn't like. Airline pilots, ballerinas, bricklayers, carpenters, clerks, coal miners, garbage collectors, movie directors, nurses, plumbers, reporters, secretaries, steel workers, university professors, and welders all joined one union. Soon about 87 percent of Poland's non-farm workforce belonged to Solidarity.

Things began to move swiftly once the union got nationally organized, and in 1980 Solidarity called a general strike demanding better pay, a 40-hour work week, more food in the stores, and official recognition of Solidarity as the bargaining agent for Polish labor (as opposed to the stooge unions Poland's communist government created). After three weeks of a non-violent work stoppage and intense international press coverage of the strike, the communist government of Poland gave in and signed an agreement for a 40-hour work week, a modest pay increase, and recognition of Solidarity's legitimacy as a negotiator for Polish workers. The government promised to make more food available.

But sixteen months later (under orders from Moscow), Poland's communist party reneged on its signed agreement and declared martial law, decreeing that an organization enrolling almost nine-tenths of the wage and salary workers in Poland was "anti-social." Every Solidarity officer the Party could round up was arrested.

The regime's decree outlawing Solidarity, however, did not destroy this unique labor union, which was also a national freedom movement. Having experienced what it felt like to stand up to tyranny and take united, non-violent action in the name of what is true and good, the people of Poland knew they had exposed the lie that Marxism serves the best interests of workers. There could be no going back to living that lie.

The Solidarity officers who escaped arrest went underground and by clandestine means continued to speak the truth about communist rule in Poland. And a few outstandingly courageous Poles like the popular young priest Jerzy Popieluszko at St. Stanislaw Kostka Church in Warsaw spoke out boldly and publicly in defiance of the martial law decree banning support for Solidarity.

Father Jerzy started conducting a "Mass for the Nation" at St. Stanislaw's the last Sunday of every month and collected money for the families of Solidarity members who were in prison. Soon attendance at these monthly religious services overflowed into the church's courtyard; then into neighboring streets. Outdoor loudspeakers had to be installed and extra priests brought in from other parishes to help distribute Communion. Father Jerzy told his countrymen who attended these Masses that the government ought to sit down and talk with representatives of Solidarity; that all Poles were brothers and sisters whether they were Christians or nonbelievers, communists or anticommunists. He prayed for Poland's healing.

When the Party could not silence the young priest through threats, government thugs kidnapped him. Eleven days later, Father Jerzy's broken and battered corpse, weighed down with rocks, was discovered in a reservoir. Hundreds of Poles were murdered during the government's crackdown on Solidarity, including two other priests. (Five more priests were abducted and beaten but not killed.[24]) The spirit of Solidarity, however, could not be eradicated. The Polish people were strong in their belief in a higher power than the Polish Workers' Party, as communists in Poland called themselves.

Year after year throughout the 1980s, Solidarity agitated for multi-party elections. Finally, in 1989, such elections were scheduled. Solidarity candidates won a landslide victory at the polls, and Lech Walesa became the president of Poland. Five months later the Berlin Wall was demolished by Germans living on both sides of it. And in December, 1991, ten years to the month after the Communist Party of Poland outlawed Solidarity, the USSR disintegrated because the legislatures of the Russian, the Byelorussian, and the Ukrainian republics had the courage to withdraw from it.

Poland's Solidarity was the most prominent and most widely inspiring of the freedom movements among the peoples of Central and Eastern Europe who liberated themselves from the iron grip of Soviet imperialism through their own sacrifices and

---

24 Grazyna Sikorska, *Jerzy Popieluszko: A Martyr for the Truth* (Eerdmans, 1985).

love of freedom. Solidarity was preceded by a series of uprisings: in East Germany in 1953; in Poland and Hungary in 1956; in Czechoslovakia in 1968 and 1977; and in Poland in 1968, 1970, and 1976. This is the compelling lesson behind the fall of the Soviet Empire. And this is the kind of sustained devotion to freedom and willingness to make sacrifices for it that Americans must have today to restore the strength of America's culture.

It is significant that the dissolution of the Soviet Union in 1989-1991 occurred halfway through *the fourth generation* after Lenin founded the Union of Soviet Socialist Republics and the Communist Party of the Soviet Union to establish Cultural Marxism in the former empire of the Russian Czars and, Lenin felt, eventually throughout the world.

CONCLUSION

No American should think the conflict between Cultural Marxism and America's culture has ended or that Cultural Marxism could never take over the United States of America. The goal of the anti-American Americans who launched what they called the Counter-Culture Movement in the 1960s was to transform America, and that remains the goal of this movement, which today is known as Political Correctness. It has progressed to the point where it has taken over most of the universities, the media, and the Democratic Party. It exerts great influence on the Republican Party and America's churches, corporations, courts, and schools. To destroy America's culture, Political Correctness is abolishing belief in self-control, redefining liberty as liberation from God's laws, and encouraging an across-the-board dependence on Big Government.

As Lincoln said in 1838, the greatest danger to America comes from within, and Political Correctness is such a danger. America's culture must be restored to make it strong enough to withstand this threat, and only those who understand what American culture is and how it is being attacked from within can accomplish that.

What is happening today and why and how it is happening must be understood before the internal enemy's claims can be effectively addressed. The claim that the Constitution of the United States means whatever federal officeholders say it means.

The claim that the Creator of all that is seen and unseen, to whom Moses and Jesus and hundreds of millions of Americans have prayed, is a "myth" (a favorite PC attack word.) And the claim that America's economy must be totally controlled ("regulated") by the four million bureaucrats the executive branch of the U.S. government currently employs.

The replacement of America's culture by Cultural Marxism can be stopped.

Appendix A

GOD'S TEN COMMANDMENTS

The American Patriot's Bible:
The Word of God and the Shaping of America
Richard G. Lee, General Editor
Nashville, Tennessee: Thomas Nelson, 2009
Exodus 20: 1-17

And God spoke all these words, saying:

"I *am* the LORD your God, who brought you out of the land of Egypt, out of the house of bondage.

"You *shall* have no other gods before Me.

"You *shall* not make for yourself a carved image—any likeness of *anything* that *is* in heaven above, or that *is* in the earth beneath, or that *is* in the water under the earth; you shall not bow down to them nor serve them. For I, the LORD your God, *am* a jealous God, visiting the iniquity of the fathers upon the children to the third and fourth *generations* of those who hate Me, but showing mercy to thousands, to those who love Me and keep My commandments.

"You *shall* not take the name of the LORD your God in vain, for the LORD will not hold *him* guiltless who takes His name in vain.

"Remember the *Sabbath day,* to keep it holy. Six days you shall labor and do all your work, but the seventh day *is* the Sabbath of the LORD your God. *In it* you shall do no work: you, nor your son, nor your daughter, nor your male servant, nor your female servant, nor your cattle, nor your stranger who is within your gates. For *in* six days the LORD made the heavens and the earth, the sea, and all that *is* in them, and rested the seventh day. Therefore the LORD blessed the Sabbath day and hallowed it.

"Honor your father and your mother, that your days may be long upon the land which the LORD your God is giving you.

"You shall not murder.

"You shall not commit adultery.

"You shall not steal.

"You shall not bear false witness against your neighbor.

"You shall not covet your neighbor's house; you shall not covet your neighbor's wife, nor his male servant, nor his female servant, nor his ox, nor his donkey, nor anything that is your neighbor's."

Appendix B

THE ARGUMENT IN THE DECLARATION OF INDEPENDENCE

The fifty-six representatives of the people of the thirteen States of the United States assembled in the Second Continental Congress in Philadelphia who approved and signed the Declaration of Independence, which was publicly proclaimed on July 4th 1776, were united in regarding the king of Britain as a tyrant and believing, as was commonly said in America in the years before and during the War for Independence, "Resistance to Tyrants Is Obedience to God." They also believed that God, the Almighty Creator of all that is, most especially the laws which govern his creations, whose effects only are visible, gives all men certain unalienable rights, including the right to life and to seek opportunities to improve their lives. Belief in God's existence is the crucial component in the proclamation of America's independence: the premise of the argument for the sovereignty of the people of the States of the United States because belief in God makes it possible to claim that human life is sacred and that human beings have rights whose origin is divine. Instead of the divine rights of kings, we have the divine rights of man.

This argument was articulated in the Declaration's first two paragraphs and its concluding paragraph.

"When in the Course of human events, it becomes necessary for one people to dissolve the political bands which have connected them with another, and to assume among the Powers of the earth, the separate and equal Station to which the Laws of Nature and of Nature's God entitle them, a decent respect to the opinions of mankind requires that they should declare the causes which impel them to the separation.

"We hold these truths to be self-evident, that all men are created equal, that they are endowed by their Creator with certain unalienable Rights, that among these are Life, Liberty and the pursuit of Happiness. That to secure these rights, Governments are instituted among Men, deriving their just powers from the consent of the governed. That whenever any Form of Government becomes destructive of these ends, it is the Right of the People to alter or to abolish it, and to institute new Government, laying its foundation on such principles and organizing its powers in such form, as to them shall seem most likely to effect their Safety and Happiness. Prudence, indeed, will dictate that Governments long established should not be changed for light and transient causes; and accordingly all experience hath shewn, that mankind are more disposed to suffer, while evils are sufferable, than to right themselves by abolishing the forms to which they are accustomed. But when a long train of abuses and usurpations, pursuing invariably the same Object evinces a design to reduce them under absolute Despotism, it is their right, it is their duty, to throw off such Government, and to provide new Guards for their future Security. Such has been the patient Sufferance of these Colonies; and such is now the necessity which constrains them to alter their former Systems of Government. The history of the present King of Great Britain is a history of repeated injuries and usurpations, all having in direct object the establishment of an absolute Tyranny over these States. To prove this, let Facts be submitted to a candid world."

[At this point in the Declaration, twenty-seven factual instances are presented of the unnatural, tyrannical conduct of the British king, George III, and the repeated failure of American efforts to recruit the support of either the British people or the British Parliament in seeking redress of their grievances.]

"WE, THEREFORE, the Representatives of the UNITED STATES OF AMERICA, in General Congress, Assembled, appealing to the Supreme Judge of the world for the rectitude of our intentions do, in the Name and by the Authority of the good People of these Colonies, solemnly publish and declare, That these United Colonies are, and of Right ought to be FREE AND INDEPENDENT STATES; that they are Absolved from all Allegiance to the British Crown, and that all political connection between them and the State of Great Britain, is and ought to be totally dissolved; and that as Free and Independent States, they have full Power to levy War, conclude Peace, contract Alliances, establish Commerce, and to do all other Acts and Things which Independent States may of right do. And for the support of this Declaration, with a firm reliance on the Protection of divine Providence, we mutually pledge to each other our Lives, our Fortunes and our sacred Honor."

The argument of the Declaration, then, comes down to this: human beings are a unique part of God's lawful, natural order ("the Laws of Nature and of Nature's God") in that the Creator has given us a special birthright and has made laws for our particular conduct which his other creatures do not have the gift of reason to comprehend or the God-given gift of freedom to obey willingly. All governments must acknowledge the natural rights the Supreme Power of the universe has bestowed on his creature man; and those which do not recognize man's unique, God-given attributes and rights but manifest over a long period of time an invariable disposition to desecrate them must be replaced.

No government may subtract from the stature which God the Almighty Creator has bestowed on human beings.

That is the gist of the argument in the Declaration of Independence.

Appendix C

THE PROFILE OF
AMERICAN CULTURE

The cultural beliefs profiled in this book are collected here for the reader's convenience.

Beliefs Regarding SOCIETY

Everyone must work and manual work is respectable.
Society is a collection of persons rather than classes.
Achievement not birth determines a person's social rank.
Everyone is responsible for imagining opportunities for their success.
Helping people who are down to get back on their feet improves society.
Organization is essential to improving society.
Freedom of movement can lead to success.

Beliefs Regarding GOVERNMENT

The people of the States have equal sovereignty.
Most persons want to do what is right, but many will abuse power.
The purpose of a written constitution is to limit the power of government.
The purpose of government is to protect liberty.
Representative government and majority rule are practical forms of justice.

Beliefs Regarding RELIGION

God created man and laws for human conduct as well as nature and its laws.
God gives all human beings the same birthright of life, freedom, the pursuit of happiness, and government by consent of the governed.
Human beings have to obey God's laws to be happy and successful.

Appendix D

THE DOGMAS OF
CULTURAL MARXISM

All human problems are material in nature and have only material solutions because human beings are only one more species of animal that has evolved on this planet by chance, without purpose or design.

The environment determines human behavior.

The purpose of government is to provide the correct social, economic, political, and material environment to achieve the well-being of every human animal.

Everyone must defer to the decisions of government experts who have the correct knowledge and necessary power to control the environment.

Any behavior which does not conform to this way of thinking is detrimental to human welfare, cannot be tolerated, and must be eliminated for the good of humanity.

TEN RECOMMENDED READINGS

The Anti-Federalists: Selected Writings & Speeches, ed. Bruce Frohnen (Regnery, 1999). Contemporary papers on the framing and ratification of the U. S. Constitution.

Carson, Ben, MD. *Gifted Hands: The Ben Carson Story,* with Cecil Murphy (Zondervan, 1990).

Franklin, Benjamin. *The Autobiography* (first published in U.S. in 1818; available in many editions).

Kimball, Roger. *The Long March: How the Cultural Revolution of the 1960s Changed America* (Encounter Books, 2000).

Madison, James. *Notes of Debates in the Federal Convention of 1787* (1840; Bicentennial Edition, W.W. Norton, 1987).

Riley, Jason L. *Please Stop Helping Us: How Liberals Make It Harder for Blacks to Succeed* (Encounter Books, 2014).

Schweikart, Larry and Michael Allen. *A Patriot's History of the United States: From Columbus's Great Discovery to the War on Terror* (Sentinel, 2004).

Vazsonyi, Balint. *America's 30 Years War: Who Is Winning?* (Regnery, 1998).

Voegeli, William. *The Pity Party: A Mean-Spirited Diatribe against Liberal Compassion* (Broadside Books, 2014).

Washington, Booker T. *Up From Slavery: An Autobiography* (1901; available in several editions).

INDEX

ABOUT THE AUTHOR

John Harmon McElroy has edited a history of Columbus, compiled a narrative of Walt Whitman's experiences in the Civil War, and authored four books on American cultural history. A professor emeritus of the University of Arizona, he also taught at Clemson University and the University of Wisconsin-Madison and as a Fulbright Professor of American Studies at universities in Spain (Salamanca) and Brazil (Santa Catarina). In the summer of 1981, he taught at the English Seminar in Poznan, Poland. He is a graduate of Princeton University with a doctorate from Duke University. He and his wife, Onyria Herrera McElroy, PhD, a writer of bilingual medical dictionaries, were married in Havana in 1957 and live in Tucson, Arizona.